THE LAW
AND THE LAWLESS

THE LAW AND THE LAWLESS

Frontier Justice in British Columbia and Yukon, 1858–1911

EDITED BY
ART DOWNS

VICTORIA · VANCOUVER · CALGARY

Heritage House Publishing Company Ltd.
heritagehouse.ca

Library and Archives Canada Cataloguing in Publication
The law and the lawless : frontier justice in British Columbia and Yukon, 1858-1911/edited by Art Downs.

(Amazing stories)
Repackaged from: Outlaws & lawmen of Western Canada.
Issued in print and electronic formats.
ISBN 978-1-927527-89-4 (pbk.).—ISBN 978-1-927527-90-0 (html).—ISBN 978-1-927527-91-7 (pdf)

1. Outlaws—British Columbia—Biography. 2. Outlaws—Yukon—Biography. 3. Police—British Columbia—Biography. 4. Police—Yukon—Biography. 5. Crime—British Columbia—History. 6. Crime—Yukon—History. 7. Frontier and pioneer life—British Columbia. 8. Frontier and pioneer life—Yukon. 9. British Columbia—History. 10. Yukon—History. I. Downs, Art, 1924-1996, editor of compilation II. Title: Frontier justice in British Columbia and Yukon, 1858-1911. III. Title: Outlaws & lawmen of Western Canada. IV. Series: Amazing stories (Victoria, B.C.)

HV6805.L38 2014   364.1092'2   C2013-908575-0   C2013-908576-9

Editor: Karla Decker
Series editor: Leslie Kenny
Proofreader: Lesley Cameron

Cover photo: North West Mounted Police detachment at Beavermouth, British Columbia, 1885. Glenbow Archives, NA-294-1.

The interior of this book was produced on 30% post-consumer recycled paper, processed chlorine free and printed with vegetable-based inks.

Heritage House acknowledges the financial support for its publishing program from the Government of Canada through the Canada Book Fund (CBF), Canada Council for the Arts and the Province of British Columbia through the British Columbia Arts Council and the Book Publishing Tax Credit.

18 17 16 15 14   1 2 3 4 5
Printed in Canada

Contents

Publisher's Note

The stories in this collection were written several decades ago and may reflect attitudes widely held at the time that would be considered unacceptable today. Where possible, we have updated the language to more contemporary standards. In the interest of historical accuracy, material quoted from archival documents is preserved in its original form.

Prologue

AS THEY TOOK THE TRAIL, *Constable Ussher told his companions that he didn't think there would be any trouble in arresting the gang. It was just after dark when they reached John McLeod's ranch. On learning their purpose, McLeod agreed to join the police party the next morning at a place called Government Camp. Soon it was apparent that they were on the right track, for at one spot in the freshly fallen snow, hoof marks led deeper into a thick patch of bush. Suddenly, in a clearing, they saw four saddled horses.*

"They'll never fire a shot," said Ussher. "Come on, I'll lead."

They had ridden but a few paces when beetle-browed Charlie McLean was noticed half-hidden behind a tree, his rifle showing. The posse reined up.

"I don't see my black horse," said Palmer.

Charlie McLean gave a sharp whistle. A shot rang out, and the bullet cut through Palmer's ice-coated beard. "That was a close one," he said, trying to control his startled horse. But the same ball had hit John McLeod. He dismounted, blood spurting from his cheeks.

Then Allan McLean was sighted taking aim from behind a tree. Palmer, armed with a shotgun, tried to get a shot at him as he dodged behind another tree. Allan fired again.

Ussher's horse, startled by the shooting, plunged and reared. Ussher slipped from the saddle. A less courageous man might have been tempted to take cover, but Ussher knew his duty, and he was a brave man. He had a revolver in his saddle holster but he left it there, perhaps thinking that his previous contact with the McLeans had earned their respect. It was a tragic misjudgment.

Ussher called on them to surrender, and then, with a deadly fusillade still going on, walked toward Alex Hare. Hare advanced, hunting knife in one hand, revolver in the other. The constable grasped the young man by the shoulder. They grappled. Hare struck repeatedly with the knife. Down went Ussher, Hare astride him. Again and again Hare used the knife, slashing Ussher in the face.

Allan McLean was heard to shout, "Kill the . . . "

Fifteen-year-old Archie darted from the shelter of a tree, revolver in hand. Holding it close to Ussher's head, he fired. Ussher lay still.

CHAPTER

1

British Columbia and Yukon's First Police Forces

BC Provincial Police

These lawmen were the first in Western Canada, their heritage dating to November 19, 1858, when the Crown Colony of British Columbia was established. Chartres Brew of the Irish Constabulary was appointed chief inspector of police; his task was formidable. That summer, some thirty thousand men had stampeded to a gold discovery on the Fraser River. They were mostly from the US, all armed with a six-gun (sometimes two), a rifle, and a bowie knife. To maintain order, Brew began with about a dozen men to police a wilderness region that didn't have a mile of road.

Larger than California, Oregon, and Washington combined, the area they patrolled extended from the

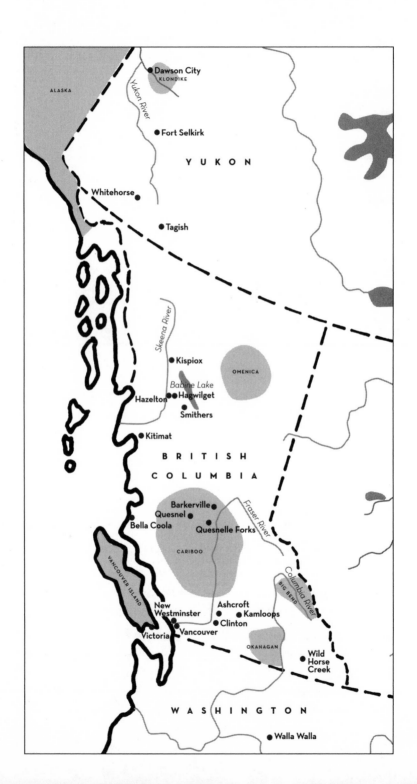

ALASKA

Dawson City
KLONDIKE

Yukon River

Fort Selkirk

Y U K O N

Whitehorse

Tagish

Skeena River

Kispiox

OMENICA

Babine Lake

Hazelton Hagwilget

Smithers

Kitimat

B R I T I S H

C O L U M B I A

Barkerville

Quesnel

Bella Coola

Quesnelle Forks

Fraser River

CARIBOO

VANCOUVER ISLAND

Columbia River

BIG BEND

New
Westminster

Ashcroft

Kamloops

Clinton

Victoria

Vancouver

OKANAGAN

Wild
Horse
Creek

W A S H I N G T O N

Walla Walla

Pacific Ocean east to the Rocky Mountains, some five hundred miles (eight hundred kilometres), from the US border to what would one day become the Yukon. During the frontier era, the new lawmen patrolled using canoe and horseback in summer, dog team and snowshoes in winter. There are many instances of them bringing prisoners more than five hundred miles by horseback, stagecoach, and canoe to a courtroom. In addition, they had to be adept with tiller and mainsail, since they also patrolled some five thousand miles (eight thousand kilometres) of coastline.

The BC Provincial Police were to serve for almost a century, from 1858 until 1950, when they were absorbed into the RCMP. In *B.C. Provincial Police Stories*, Deputy Commissioner Cecil Clark wrote:

> These far-ranging police officers saw not only the coming of the telegraph, the telephone and electric light but also were on duty when the four-horse stagecoach gave way to the train, the automobile and the airplane. They readily embraced anything new that would make them more efficient and were proud that their experiments enabled them to establish the first city-to-city, short-wave police radio communication system in North America.
>
> Whether assisting victims of fire or flood or merely performing the daily routine of urban duty, these British Columbia policemen did it with pride born of a sense of history. Thirteen died in the performance of their duty, expecting nothing more than that they be remembered.

The North West Mounted Police (NWMP)

This force, today's RCMP, was born in 1873, when the vast wilderness between Manitoba and the Rocky Mountains was called the North-West Territories. It was a lawless land where US whisky traders were rapidly wiping out the Plains tribes. Stamping out this whisky trade was the prime reason for the formation of the new police force. In 1874, the force assembled at Dufferin, Manitoba, and began an 800-mile-long trek (1,290 kilometres) west. The officers built Fort Macleod, the first NWMP post, and in 1875 established Fort Calgary. The force's duties included maintaining law and order during the construction of the Canadian Pacific Railway in the early 1880s, and later it was responsible for the thousands of settlers flooding the West. In 1890, the NWMP were given another massive responsibility: Arctic Canada. The first force of nineteen men arrived in Yukon in 1895, and when the discovery of gold in 1896 resulted in fifty thousand men stampeding north in 1897–98, the Mounties upheld their motto, "Maintain the Right."

In 1899, in one of Yukon's most brutal crimes, three men were murdered, and then snow covered the evidence. But brilliant police work by several NWMP officers helped to track the fugitives and bring them to justice.

In 1904, as a reward for the dedicated service performed by the North West Mounted Police, King Edward VII conferred the prefix "Royal" to their name. In 1920, the name was changed to the Royal Canadian Mounted Police (RCMP).

2

Western Canada's Pioneer Lawmen

ONE ASPECT OF BRITISH COLUMBIA'S HISTORY is the refreshing lack of gunfighters in the province's otherwise colourful past. There was no Billy the Kid, Wyatt Earp, or Wild Bill Hickock, although there should have been. At the province's birth in 1858, all the ingredients that would encourage such characters were present.

That spring, word reached San Francisco that gold had been found to the north on a river that few, if any, locals had heard of. The river was the Fraser, known mainly to the Native people and fur traders of the Hudson's Bay Company (HBC). For their part, Company officials not only were satisfied that the region was unknown but also deliberately discouraged settlement, knowing that farming and fur trading were a poor mixture. Unfortunately for the HBC, on a Sunday morning in April, the paddlewheel steamer *Commodore* appeared off Fort Victoria at the southern tip of Vancouver Island. Some five hundred hopeful gold seekers disembarked, followed in the next few months by over thirty thousand more. The quiet fur-trading post was suddenly a jamboree of tents. Land that previously couldn't find a buyer at five dollars an acre was soon $3,000 an acre. Stores, hotels, and saloons appeared, providing the perfect setting for gunfighters (particularly the saloons).

Furthermore, there was no shortage of rifles or revolvers. Wrote author Kinahan Cornwallis of one miner, "He was a gaunt, stringy, dried-up looking Kentuckian, with a gutta-percha face, sunk into which . . . twinkled two all alive and piercing eyes . . . He carried a couple of revolvers, and a bowie knife, with the point of which he took the opportunity of picking his teeth immediately after supper."

Another writer in June 1858 noted of the Americans, "They were all . . . equipped with the universal revolver, many of them carrying a brace of such, as well as a bowie knife."

Most of the incoming miners were law-abiding, but other men were not. They were the outlaws, many of them chased from American mining camps by vigilante committees. But when these renegades arrived at the tent town of Fort Victoria, ready to acquire gold by means other than mining, they received a shock. A month after the first swarm of miners stepped ashore, a local ordinance banned the belt gun, and that was that. Potential Billy the Kids and Wild Bill Hickocks never had a chance to flourish.

One thug whose potential crime career was blunted in Victoria was Boone Helm—and he was a true thug. Gunfighter, murderer, thief, he had robbed stages, bribed judges and juries, and cold-bloodedly killed a partner whose only offence was that he had agreed to go to California with Helm and then changed his mind. Helm was also a cannibal. Once, on a trip from Walla Walla (in today's Washington) to Salt Lake City, he subsisted for a week on the leg of a dead companion. (For a detailed telling of the story of Boone Helm, see chapter 3.)

By 1864, massive changes had occurred in the former HBC fur preserve. Although sand and gravel bars on the Fraser River had in 1858–59 yielded millions in gold, the ever-restless miners surged upstream. Some four hundred miles (six hundred and forty kilometres) to the north, at the headwaters of one of the river's major tributaries, they uncovered the motherlode. The region became known as the Cariboo, and by 1865 was to yield some $50 million— with gold selling at sixteen dollars an ounce.

Despite this treasure, which attracted men good and bad from around the world, the region was remarkably law-abiding. In 1862, a correspondent for *The Times* newspaper in London wrote, "As to security of life, I consider it just as safe here as in England."

The reason dated back to 1849, when Vancouver Island

was proclaimed a crown colony and the existing laws of England applied. A judge was appointed, but with a population of under a hundred, there was no crime. If there were some recalcitrant Indigenous people up the coast, the governor, James Douglas, sent a gunboat to shell them, and that was that. An exception took place in 1852, when the HBC's *Beaver*, the first steam vessel on the Pacific Coast, was used as a courtroom for the first jury ever assembled in the West. Two Native people were found guilty of murdering a shepherd and hanged the next morning.

At the time of the gold rush of 1858, Governor Douglas appointed Augustus C. Pemberton as commissioner of police, the first in the two-thousand-mile wide (over three-thousand-kilometre) region that became Western Canada. Working under him were Superintendent Horace Smith and about a dozen constables. Although all were unarmed, they quickly established themselves as peacekeepers.

Take one gang called the Forty Thieves, which had terrorized San Francisco. Lured by the new gold strike, several gang members ventured north. All were rounded up within a week and shipped back. Perhaps the presence of Constable Joe Eden hastened their peaceful exit. He was a prizefighter, and in those days, it was straight bare knuckles, with a fight lasting until the opponent was unconscious or surrendered. One of Joe's triumphs over a challenger named George Baker lasted nearly two hours and went for 128 rounds. Joe won $500 and the next day was back on duty.

The police force formed by Governor Douglas and A. Pemberton, however, had jurisdiction only on Vancouver Island. The task of organizing the second group of lawmakers in Western Canada fell to an Irishman named Chartres Brew. In 1858, he was appointed by Britain's Secretary of State for the Colonies, Sir Edward Bulwer-Lytton, to organize a force to keep order in the new gold colony. Brew had already served with distinction in the Crimean War and had fourteen years' experience in the Royal Irish Constabulary. An item in *The Victoria Gazette* in November 1858 noted: "The steamer *Beaver* . . . sailed for Fort Langley yesterday morning. She had on board Captain Grant and his company of Royal Engineers, and Captain Brew, the new commissioner of police for British Columbia. It is the intention of Captain Brew to organize an efficient force in the new colony immediately . . . "

Brew's first problem, the item continued, was the scarcity of suitable men for the force.

"It will be extremely difficult to find men in British Columbia fit for the police. The class of men who now offer themselves for enrollment are, with few exceptions, persons not to be trusted as peace officers.

"They are chiefly miners who would never become obedient subordinates or submit themselves to the strict discipline which must always be maintained in an armed corps.

"These men, besides, merely want employment for the

winter months and are determined to return to their mining pursuits on the opening of spring, so that just when they know something of their duties and their services were most needed they would abandon the force."

Brew asked Governor Douglas to send for members of the Royal Irish Constabulary, in the meantime enrolling men he felt would fulfill the awesome responsibility. The measure of his success was summarized by Northwest historian H.H. Bancroft, who wrote, "Never in the pacification and settlement of any section of America have there been so few disturbances, so few crimes against law and order."

The policemen were very thinly spread, and many instances are recorded in which they had to transport their prisoners by horseback, stagecoach, or canoe for hundreds of miles. They were to police British Columbia for nearly a century, until the RCMP took over provincial law-enforcement duties.

In the pioneer days of the force, the constables evolved their own way of dealing with rowdies. Since they didn't have to contend with defence lawyers, the policemen could be original in their method of peacekeeping. Take Jack Kirkup, who stood six feet, three inches (one hundred and ninety centimetres) and weighed three hundred pounds (one hundred and thirty-six kilograms).

BC historian Elsie G. Turnbull wrote of him:

Constable Kirkup treated the unruly element with a heavy hand. His method of control consisted of "pounding instead of impounding offenders." A typical instance concerned the visit of a hairy-chested tough from Kaslo to Revelstoke in the Arrow-Kootenay Lakes region of B.C. This man was in the habit of shaking dice in a saloon and if he won would shake again. If he lost he would refuse to pay. He would laugh, stroll away and call out: "That's the way we do things in Kaslo!"

One saloon-keeper, in anger, hit him with a two-by-four, and a crowd gathered. Kirkup waited until the man regained consciousness, but instead of arresting him, took him to the edge of town. Here he started the dice-shaker off toward Kaslo with the words: "Tell 'em in Kaslo that's the way we do things in Revelstoke."

In his "pounding instead of impounding" policy, Kirkup was aided by a walking cane presented by an ex-convict. Made of leather and silver-trimmed, it not only looked pretty but was functional too, since it had an embedded steel rod and weighted butt. As Elsie Turnbull observed, "Wielded by the powerful constable it became a lethal weapon that effectively quietened any potential disturber of the peace."

Kirkup's answer to drunkenness was to lock up the drunk and then go after the saloon keeper. "Many a bartender learned to keep his difficult customers out of sight until they were normal again," Tumbull noted. "Kirkup sometimes encouraged 'tanked' miners to fight, believing a little exercise would help work the whiskey out of their pores. If men were long on talk and short on performance it wasn't unknown for Kirkup to bump heads together until he got them mad and then set them down to finish it."

Then there is the story of a boxing match in Rossland staged by two shysters from Spokane. Unfortunately for them, Kirkup was chosen to referee. Knowing that they had been faking their bouts, he brought them together in the ring. "Boys," he said quietly, "I don't want to see any flim flam here. I want to see a spirited exhibition. And to ensure that it is, the loser's going to get three months in jail."

While Kirkup's peacekeeping methods were perhaps unorthodox, they achieved their objective. But the thinly spread policemen had formidable allies, especially during the force's formative years. These allies were judges such as John Carmichael Haynes, Peter O'Reilly, and Matthew Baillie Begbie. They rode enormous distances while performing their duties, holding court in log cabins, tents, and even astride their saddle horses.

J.C. Haynes was twenty-seven when he landed in British Columbia in 1858 to join Brew's police force. In 1860, he was appointed deputy collector of customs in the Okanagan-Similkameen region of southern BC, and in 1864, Justice of the Peace. Like other frontier justices, he travelled on horseback, identified by his Irish frieze jacket, well-cut riding breeches, and polished English riding boots. In summer he wore a pith helmet, in winter a more practical felt hat, but

BC Policeman Jack Kirkup in 1884. A powerful man, Kirkup believed in "pounding instead
of impounding" cheats, thugs, and others
who preyed on honest citizens. HERITAGE HOUSE

never a Stetson, which he considered undignified. Quiet, well informed, and gentlemanly, wherever he went he was the law.

Shortly after his appointment in 1864, Haynes set out with Constable Young from the Okanagan for the new mining community of Wild Horse Creek in the shadow of the Rocky Mountains, some three hundred miles (four hundred and eighty kilometres) east. After twenty days in the saddle, they reached Wild Horse, a community of some fifty cabins, a few dance halls and gambling joints, and a brewery. The day before Haynes arrived, it had also been the scene of a blazing gunfight that left one man dead and one badly wounded.

Gold had been discovered at Wild Horse Creek the year before, and in the area were upwards of two thousand miners—most heavily armed. The only law was of the home-made variety, a type of vigilante committee led by Robert Dore. There were two factions in the camp. The majority were US citizens, led by a trio named "Yeast Powder" Bill Burmister, "Overland" Bob Evans, and Neil Dougherty. The Canadian minority was headed by a fiery and vocal young Irishman, Thomas Walker. The two groups met on the hot afternoon of August 9 in front of the Fortier Cafe.

An argument erupted, and Walker pulled his revolver. He fired point-blank at Yeast Powder Bill but, unfortunately for Walker, he only shot the end off Yeast Powder's thumb. Before Walker could fire again, the American drew one of his two guns with his undamaged hand. He pulled the trigger, and Walker dropped, a bullet in his heart.

Overland Bob Evans then started shooting, and a free-for-all ensued. When the fracas ended, casualties included Overland Bob, who was so badly wounded that he spent three months recovering, a man named Kelly, who was stabbed in the back, and another called Paddy Skie, clubbed so hard that he was unconscious for months.

An account of subsequent events was written by D.M. Drumheller in his book, *"Uncle Dan" Drumheller Tells Thrills of Western Trails*:

> A mob was quickly raised by the friends of Tommy Walker for the purpose of hanging Overland Bob and Yeast Powder Bill. Then a law and order organization numbering about 1,000 miners, of which I was a member, assembled. It was the purpose of our organization to order a miners' court and give all concerned a fair trial. Our organization took care of the . . . wounded men and put a strong guard around them. The next morning we appointed a lawyer by the name of A.J. Gregory as trial judge and John McClellan sheriff, with authority to appoint as many deputies as he wished. That was the condition of things when Judge Haines (Haynes), the British Columbia Commissioner, rode into camp.
>
> "Fifteen hundred men under arms in the queen's dominion. A dastardly usurpation of authority, don't cher know," remarked Judge Haines. But one little English constable with knee breeches, red cap, cane in his hand, riding a jockey saddle and mounted on a bob-tailed horse, quelled that mob in 15 minutes.

Haynes relieved the "sheriff" of further duties and held an inquest. Although the jury was confused about who shot whom in the gun duel, they felt that Yeast Powder Bill had acted in self-defence. A subsequent preliminary hearing agreed, and Yeast Powder Bill was set free.

* * *

It was inevitable that a price would be paid by those responsible for maintaining everything "quiet and orderly." Near the community of Bella Coola on the British Columbia coast, on May 6, 1865, the eighty-ton trading schooner *Langley* swung at anchor in a little bay. Forward, in the ship's fo'c'sle, an oil lamp swinging in a gimbal cast eerie shadows as Skipper Smith poked some wood in the stove preparatory to making coffee. Nearby on a locker sat big, bearded BC Police Constable J.D.B. "Jack" Ogilvie, sole representative of the law between Cape Caution and the Skeena River—two hundred miles (three hundred and twenty kilometres) as the crow flies, but several thousand along the fjords that characterize the region.

As the men talked, they didn't notice the door of the forward chain locker slowly open. From it peered a crafty, evil-looking face, thin, unshaven, with eyes deep set and treacherous. The man behind the face—thirty-five-year-old French-Canadian Antoine Lucanage—raised a heavy Colt revolver, levelled it at the unsuspecting police officer, and pulled the trigger.

The crashing report rocked the little cabin. In an acrid,

billowing cloud of black-powder smoke, Ogilvie got slowly to his feet and then slumped down. Skipper Smith, with one quick glance at the gunman's hideout, fled up the companionway to the deck. There he found Morris Moss, a coastal fur trader and Ogilvie's friend.

A few days earlier, Ogilvie had asked Moss to help him capture some renegade white people who were selling liquor to the Natives. Chief among them was Antoine Lucanage, who, on April 1, 1865, in broad daylight boldly sailed right into Bella Coola. He and his boat were seized by Ogilvie, and Lucanage was shipped to jail at New Westminster on a passing schooner.

On the way, he jumped overboard at the south end of Johnstone Strait and, despite swirling tide rips, miraculously reached shore. He was later picked up by the *Langley*, whose skipper was unaware that Lucanage was on his way to jail. By a strange quirk of fate, Bella Coola was among her stopping places. At Bella Coola, Lucanage slipped ashore at night. When Ogilvie heard of the incident, he mustered some Native people and searched the area, but found no trace of the fugitive.

A couple of days later, when the *Langley* left, Ogilvie had a hunch that Lucanage had somehow regained the vessel. "Let's catch her up and search her," was his quick suggestion to Moss.

With six swiftly paddling Native people, the pair set off and about four hours later caught the schooner. Her skipper,

Smith, swore that the fugitive wasn't aboard. Ten minutes later came the dramatic moment when Lucanage fired the shot from the chain locker.

Smith rushed up on deck to incoherently tell his story to Moss, who promptly grabbed a lantern to go down into the fo'c'sle after the gunman. At that moment, however, Ogilvie staggered up on deck. Then Lucanage appeared, knife in one hand, revolver in the other.

Constable Ogilvie, though mortally wounded, grappled with the cutthroat and wrested the gun from him. Then, as Lucanage turned and ran toward a companionway, Ogilvie fired two shots at him. Moss, aft at the wheel, drew his revolver and ran forward, but the mainsail boom swung over and hurled him into the water. The Natives in the canoe heard him yell and picked him up.

When Moss got back on board, he noticed that Ogilvie was near total collapse. He and Smith packed the wounded man below, and as they were doing so, Lucanage escaped in a skiff. Below deck, Ogilvie lived only a few more minutes.

The murder stirred the colony, and the government offered a $1,000 reward for Lucanage's capture. Despite the reward and a protracted search, he was never found alive, although he was variously reported as far south as San Francisco. Finally, several months later, a corpse was found on northern Vancouver Island and identified as Lucanage. One story is that he had escaped with the aid of Native canoemen and promised them blankets in return. Once on

On May 6, 1865, John D.B. Ogilvie became
the first lawman murdered in British Columbia.
BRITISH COLUMBIA ARCHIVES B-00460

Vancouver Island, he had tried to escape without paying
his debt and the Natives killed him. Had they known of the
reward, they could have been $1,000 richer.

A similar type of justice avenged the second policeman
to die on duty. After Judge J.C. Haynes journeyed to Wild

Horse Creek in 1864 to bring law and order, three constables were subsequently stationed there. They were James Carrington, Jimmy Normansell, and Jack Lawson, a young man from New Brunswick.

In 1867, while Normansell and Carrington were on patrol, two Dutch ranchers rode into Wild Horse and reported that their horses had been stolen and that they had tracked the thief to a camp about four miles (six and a half kilometres) away. Lawson accompanied the two back to the camp, and after about an hour spotted the thief coming down the trail.

The constable stopped him, and as he asked about the horses, he noticed the man's hand slipping inside his jacket. Lawson promptly drew his gun and gave curt instructions to get his hands in the air. Lawson then turned to call one of the ranchers forward—a split-second error that cost him his life. With a lightning draw, the thief put a bullet through the back of the policeman's head. As the hapless constable reeled in the saddle and slipped to the ground, it was the cue for the Dutchmen to spur their horses. The thief coolly took the constable's gun and then left in the opposite direction.

The man who had murdered Lawson was Charlie "One Ear" Brown, well known to Victoria police. His first conviction in the community had occurred on November 3, 1859, for peddling whisky. After a spell at hard labour, which consisted of tamping rocks to hard-surface the young community's streets while wearing leg irons, he was freed—but not for long. He was soon back on the chain gang for swindling a Native person. In 1861, he was back twice; the second time, he received a one-year sentence and a nickname, "One Ear," that would later considerably help the cause of justice.

The nickname was born one afternoon when jailer Charles B. Wright got orders to move Brown to another cell. When Wright entered the cell, Brown backed against the wall and muttered, "You lay a hand on me, you son of a bitch, and I'll murder you."

In the ensuing struggle, Brown got a headlock on the jailer, but Wright managed to draw his gun. Working the muzzle close to Brown's ear, he gave a crisp order: "Let go, or I'll blow your head off."

In reply, Brown increased the pressure. Wright squeezed the trigger. Brown was fortunate that he lost only his ear; in return, he gained a nickname and another year on the street gang for assaulting a peace officer. He soon tired of tamping rocks, however, and feigned illness to get into hospital. Two days later he escaped, believed to be headed for the Cariboo. Instead, he did a little horse stealing in the Fraser Valley and then heard about the riches at Wild Horse Creek. He headed eastward via the US, continuing his horse stealing, as the two Dutch ranchers knew from first-hand experience.

After One Ear Brown shot Lawson and headed for the border, the ranchers galloped back to Wild Horse. In the absence of the policemen, they told their story to a silent and grim-eyed group of miners. Four of them exchanged glances and broke away from the group. They saddled up, made sure their shotguns were loaded, and left to avenge the murder.

They discovered that One Ear had crossed the St. Mary's River on a raft and had lost most of his supplies in the rough water. Next, they reined their sweating horses at Joe Davis's camp, where they learned that the lop-eared bandit had got some grub. Some distance farther on, the four vigilantes came on a lone Chinese person. Yes, he had seen a man. Yes, he had a missing ear. He had wanted ammunition, but the Chinese man didn't have any.

On they pressed, next checking with a blacksmith, who said the earless fugitive had got some grub from him. He was still armed, and boastfully recounted how he'd killed a BC policeman and was going to shoot a couple of Dutchmen as soon as he got the chance. Not long afterward, the self-appointed lawmen reached the Idaho border but dispensed with the formalities of a legal crossing. As they neared Bonner's Ferry, they met a Native man who told them he had been accosted by a horseman—a man minus one ear, who wanted ammunition. It was then the four miners realized that they had outrun their quarry and, if they circled back, could cut him off.

The result was reported later in the *British Columbian* newspaper at New Westminster:

Leaving their jaded horses at the ferry, and disguising themselves with moccasins, etc., they pushed forward . . . and lay in wait for him. Seeing no footprints of either man or beast on the trail, Brown pressed on, thinking himself safe. They soon saw him advancing at a rapid pace, with a remaining pistol in one hand and a knife in the other. Three of them raised their double-barrelled guns, loaded with buckshot, and fired simultaneously, literally riddling his dastardly carcass. Returning the following day, they dug a hole into which they put the remains of Charles Brown, the thief and cowardly murderer. He lies close by the side of Walla Walla trail, 43 miles south of the boundary line.

Since the episode happened across the border, British Columbia's reputation of never having had a murderer disposed of by vigilantes remained unsullied.

* * *

While events leading to the tragic murder of Constable Lawson were unfurling, Judge J.C. Haynes's duties at Wild Horse had been assumed by another Irishman, Peter O'Reilly. He came to British Columbia in 1858 and in April 1859 was appointed assistant gold commissioner, then stipendiary magistrate. In forthcoming years, he served in many regions where gold was discovered, including the Cariboo, Omineca, Big Bend, and Wild Horse Creek. At Wild Horse he gave an address that has become a British Columbian legend.

Since there was no stenographer to record his words, there are many versions of what he said. Possibly the most accurate is in a book called *Fifteen Years' Sport and Life in the Hunting Grounds of Western America and British Columbia*, written by W.A. Baillie-Grohman, a sportsman-developer who arrived in the East Kootenay in 1882. According to Baillie-Grohman, when O'Reilly arrived at Wild Horse, he addressed a group of miners in front of "the single-roomed cabin which he had turned into a temporary courthouse . . . and made a famous speech which is still remembered throughout the mining camps . . . Standing near the pole from which floated the Union Jack . . . he said: 'Boys, I am here to keep order and to administer the law. Those who don't want law and order can "git," but those who stay with the camp, remember on what side of the line the camp is; for, boys, if there is shooting in Kootenay there will be hanging in Kootenay.'"

The only problem with the address is that some authors attribute it to Judge Haynes. In his book, however, Baillie-Grohman notes, "Two old miners, Clark and Doyle, who were present on the occasion, gave me this version of Judge O'Reilly's speech. It varies but triflingly from [historian H.H.] Bancroft's version. When I asked Mr. O'Reilly for the real version, he told me he had long forgotten the exact words he had used."

Support for O'Reilly being the originator—and also an indication of the respect accorded him by the miners—is contained in another book, *Ocean to Ocean*. It is an account of an 1872 expedition across Canada led by Sandford Fleming, the Canadian Pacific Railway's engineer-in-chief.

On October 1, 1872, at Ashcroft Manor, the expedition's secretary, Reverend G.M. Grant, wrote:

> This evening we met Judge O'Reilly, whose praises had been often sung by Brown and Beaupre [packers and ex-miners hired near Fort Edmonton to care for the expedition's packhorses]. "There isn't the gold in British Columbia that would bribe Judge O'Reilly," was their emphatic endorsement of his dealings with the miners. They described him, arriving as the representative of British law and order, at Kootenie [one of many variations in the spelling of "Kootenay"], immediately after thousands had flocked to the newly discovered gold mines there. Assembling them, he said that order must and would be kept; and advised them not to display their revolvers unnecessarily, "for, boys, if there's shooting in Kootenie, there will be hanging . . . "

Three days after meeting Judge O'Reilly, Fleming's expedition boarded the sternwheel steamer *Onward* at Yale and met another judge, Matthew Baillie Begbie, the most famous of all British Columbia's lawmen. Reverend Grant wrote:

> On board the "Onward" we met Chief Justice Begbie, another man held in profound respect by the miners, Siwashes, and all others among whom he has dealt out justice. Judge Lynch has never been required in British Columbia, because Chief Justice Begbie did his duty . . . It is a grand sight to see . . . a British judge backed by one or two constables maintaining order at the gold mines among the . . . gamblers, claim "jumpers" and cutthroats who congregate at such places . . .

Like Police Inspector Chartres Brew, Begbie had been selected by Sir Edward Bulwer-Lytton to help maintain order in British Columbia. Since the new judge had to spend weeks in the saddle because there were no roads in the hundreds of miles of wilderness, Lytton wanted a young, athletic man. He also, in Lytton's own words, "must be a man who could, if necessary, truss a murderer up and hang him from the nearest tree."

Begbie arrived in British Columbia on November 16, 1858, and three days later was appointed judge, the only one in a region that covered an area larger than most of Europe. It was a dramatic change for a man who, a few months before, was a struggling barrister in England. While he personally never had to "truss a murderer up and hang him from the nearest tree," he quickly established a record for fearlessness and impartial justice.

For instance, in a saloon at Williams Lake in the Cariboo during the gold rush, a US citizen named Gilchrist attempted to shoot a man named Turner. But as Gilchrist pulled the trigger, someone bumped him, and the bullet killed a man leaning on the bar, fast asleep.

As Dr. W.W. Walkem noted in his book, *Stories of Early British Columbia*:

> The case subsequently came before Judge Begbie, and a jury chosen from a class of people composed of many fugitives from justice from the American side, and known to be horse thieves from The Dalles, Oregon. [In the early days of the

gold rush there were seldom enough British subjects for a jury, and US residents were sworn in—without too many questions asked.]

After a very patient hearing of the evidence . . . Judge Begbie charged the jury very strongly against the prisoner, at the same time severely condemning the carrying of weapons of a dangerous and deadly character. He warned the jury against being carried away by sympathy, or by the accidental nature of the shooting. The prisoner in attempting to kill one man had killed another. That was murder . . .

The jury retired, and after an absence of thirty minutes returned with a verdict of "manslaughter." Turning to the prisoner, the chief justice said: " . . . It is far from a pleasant duty for me to have to sentence you only to imprisonment for life. I feel I am, through some incomprehensible reason, prevented from doing my proper duty . . . Your crime was unmitigated, diabolical murder. You deserve to be hanged! Had the jury performed their duty I might now have the painful satisfaction of condemning you to death, and you, gentlemen of the jury, you are a pack of Dalles horse thieves, and permit me to say, it would give me great pleasure to see you hanged, each and every one of you, for declaring a murderer guilty only of manslaughter.

Another incident involved an Irishman named Davie Lavin, who was charged with murder following a fist fight with Johnston Robertson in Victoria's Regent Saloon. Robertson died three days later of brain injuries. The jury felt that Lavin was not totally responsible, since Robertson had been involved in several other fights during the afternoon. They decided that one additional punch wasn't necessarily the cause of death and acquitted Lavin.

Begbie was furious at the verdict:

> Gentlemen of the Jury . . . I have heard your verdict. But mind you, it's your verdict, not mine. On your conscience will rest the stigma of returning such a disgraceful verdict and one at variance with the evidence on which you have sworn to find the guilt or innocence of the prisoner. Many repetitions of such conduct as yours will make trial by jury a horrible farce and the city of Victoria, which you inhabit, a nest of immorality and crime encouraged by immunity from the law which criminals will receive from the announcement of such verdicts as yours. I have nothing more to say to you.

Begbie then turned to Lavin. "Prisoner, you are discharged! Go, and sandbag some of the jurymen! They deserve it!"

But not only errant jurors felt Begbie's wrath; lawbreakers quickly learned that the judge had little sympathy for them. During the spring assizes in 1861, a man named John Burke received nine months' hard labour for stealing two pairs of blankets. Two Chinese people found guilty of stealing a pistol got two years' hard labour.

In addition to a jail term, Begbie frequently imposed a flogging with the dreaded "cat-o'-nine-tails." Police Inspector Chartres Brew objected to flogging, but Begbie defended it in a letter to Governor Douglas: "My idea is that if a man insists on behaving like a brute, after a fair warning, & won't quit the Colony; treat him like a brute & flog him."

(While this statement may give the impression that Begbie was merciless, he really wasn't. He disliked imposing the death penalty, but it was the law and he had no choice. Flogging was also the law, and remained so in Canada until about 1930.)

Begbie's stern insistence that everyone obey the law or pay the penalty soon built him a reputation for impartiality and firmness. On one occasion, after a shooting escapade, miners themselves apprehended those involved and held them, knowing Begbie would arrive as soon as he learned of the incident. He held court wherever convenient: a settler's cabin, a barn, a tent, or even while sitting on his horse, always properly dressed in his robes and wig.

The result of Begbie's firmness was noted in the *Victoria Colonist* on August 17, 1863, in a news report on the absence of crime around the Cariboo goldfields: "Everything is very quiet and orderly on (Williams) Creek owing in great measure to Mr. O'Reilly's efficiency and the wholesome presence of Judge Begbie who seems to be a terror to evil doers and a sworn enemy to the use of the knife and revolver. Crime in Cariboo has been vigorously checked in its infancy by a firm hand, and seems to have sought some soil more congenial to its growth . . . "

Judge Begbie would continue to dispense justice with his

"firm hand" for over thirty years after that newspaper item. In 1870, he was saddened by the sudden death of Chartres Brew, the province's first policeman. In 1867, Brew had been transferred to Cariboo as magistrate and gold commissioner, with headquarters at Barkerville. But the harsh climate of the mountains and deplorable living conditions while travelling the district affected his health, and he died at fifty-five.

On his grave in Barkerville is the following epitaph, written by Judge Begbie: "A man imperturbable in courage and temper, endowed with a great & varied administrative capacity, a most ready wit, a most pure integrity, and a most humane heart." Begbie also described the harsh conditions endured by Brew and other judicial officials while on circuit, living in a tent and cooking over an open fire:

> The climate in Cariboo is at times exceedingly wet, as in all high mountainous regions—and it is not unusual to have torrents of rain for a week . . . almost without intermission. The tent being the same as my own—and although it answers very well in tolerable weather or even for a few days of rain, and where the camp is changed from time to time, I find that my tent becomes occasionally covered with mildew in the inside while it is impossible to keep books etc. dry, and all writing & recording is carried on at the greatest inconvenience. Besides, the ground being constantly cold & damp, and there being no opportunity of approaching a fire without going out into the heavy rain, all cooking, or drying any articles of apparel becomes extremely irksome; and all

officers who have to remain for any length of time in that district ought to (be provided) at least with one room having a fireplace where they may at least be sure to meet a dry place to lie on, and the means of warming themselves and drying their clothes, keeping their books etc. and placing a table so to be able to write.

The same year that Brew died, Begbie was appointed chief justice of the Crown Colony of British Columbia, and when BC joined Confederation in 1871, chief justice of the Province of British Columbia. He continued his career for over twenty years after Confederation, becoming Sir Matthew Baillie Begbie and hearing his last case on May 1, 1894, when he was seventy-five. A little over a month later, he died. Although the judge wished for a quiet funeral, such was his reputation that the provincial government decreed he was to have a state funeral. One of the pallbearers was Premier Theodore Davie, and among the mourners, Peter O'Reilly, who had become a close friend. In his excellent biography of Begbie, *The Man For a New Country,* author David R. Williams notes that "Victoria has not since witnessed a funeral equal to it."

Of assessments made about the chief justice, a miner wrote the most unorthodox when he noted, "Begbie was the biggest man, the smartest man, the best looking man, and the damndest man that ever came over the Cariboo road."

While Begbie probably would have considered the tribute too flattering, he would undoubtedly have agreed that

Judge Matthew Baillie Begbie, "the biggest man, the smartest man, the best looking man, and the damndest man that ever came over the Cariboo road." HERITAGE HOUSE

much of it also applied to Police Inspector Chartres Brew and his few constables, to Judge Haynes and Judge O'Reilly, and to all other pioneer lawmen who maintained order in a frontier land.

3

Boone Helm—
The Murdering Cannibal

WHO WAS THE MOST VICIOUS criminal to brutalize his way through the pioneer history of the North American West? Popular contenders include Billy the Kid, Jesse James, and the controversial Sheriff Henry Plummer, who was hanged in the Idaho Territory in 1864 by vigilantes who claimed this villain had murdered over a hundred people. These candidates all paled in comparison to Boone Helm. He became widely known as the Kentucky Cannibal as he terrorized California, Oregon, Washington Territory, and the crown colonies of Vancouver Island and British Columbia.

"Worst of the bad men, wildest of the wild bunch; depraved and bestial was Boone Helm," was how Western historian Hoffman Birney painted Helm in his book *Vigilantes*.

The 19th-century historian Nathaniel P. Langford wrote of Helm, "He was a hideous monster of depravity, whom neither precept nor example could have saved from a life of crime."

Helm arrived at Victoria in October 1862 but quickly experienced the difference between conditions in the British colony and most mining settlements in the American west. This difference was law and order. To his astonishment, Helm—who had murdered with knife and gun and had eaten at least one of his victims—found himself in jail—for the first time—a few hours after he set foot ashore, for stealing a few apples and refusing to pay for his drinks at a local saloon.

That his reputation had preceded him was evident from a report of his arrest published in Victoria's *Colonist* newspaper. Victoria's citizens probably wondered what had attracted so unsavoury a person to the peaceful streets of their city. The answer was that the Cariboo gold rush on the mainland was in full flourish, and gold by the ton was coming from the creeks some six hundred miles (a thousand kilometres) to the northeast. That was incentive enough for Helm—not that he had any intention of doing honest work; stealing and murdering were his specialties.

Helm was now thirty-four. He had been born in Kentucky and developed into an illiterate, wild, and rowdy tough. He could ride as soon as he could walk, was never without a weapon of some kind, and was an expert knife

42

thrower. Often he would drive the blade of his knife into the ground from a horse, and, returning at a gallop, stoop from the saddle and retrieve it. On one occasion, when a sheriff was looking for him, he rode his horse into the courtroom to inquire what he was wanted for.

He married in 1848 but abandoned his wife a year later. It was the year his imagination was stirred by news of the California gold rush. He rode over to his friend Littlebury Shoot's place to ask if he would go with him, but Shoot couldn't because of family commitments. It was the last decision Shoot made. In a rage, Helm stabbed him to death with a bowie knife. It was Helm's first murder, senseless and brutal, the first of many.

Helm escaped, but a reward notice appeared in the *Jefferson City Inquirer* on September 20, 1851. He was described as about " . . . five feet ten to eleven inches high— tolerably heavy built, weight from 165 to 175 pounds—from 22 to 25 years old; determined countenance and appearance, fair complexion, blue eyes . . . "

He was captured in a Native camp and returned to Munro County, Missouri, for the murder of his friend. Feigning insanity, he was judged insane and locked up. A few weeks later he escaped and headed west. It was the last Missouri saw of him, its citizens little realizing how fortunate they were.

The West saw plenty of him, though. He turned up in California, but not as a miner. There were easier ways of making a living. Sometimes, when there was objection to his thieving habits, he killed the complainant. Lightning-quick on the draw, his killings were always made to look like self-defence. Finally, he overstepped himself when he shot a miner in the back. As the record has it, "at length he committed actual murder."

California now too hot for him, he made his way north to The Dalles, Oregon, in 1858, the year gold was discovered on the Fraser River in what would become British Columbia. Gold was also discovered in what is today Utah, Nevada, and Idaho, and Helm decided to go there.

For protection from hostile Native people, most travellers crossed the Pacific Northwest in groups. Helm and a companion, Elijah Burton, joined a party heading for Camp Floyd, Utah, sixty miles (ninety-seven kilometres) southwest of Salt Lake City. They were to go by way of Fort Hall on the Snake River, a trip of over five hundred miles (eight hundred kilometres) through rough country and with constant danger of attack. Helm's party met with so many obstacles that they returned to The Dalles.

That fall, Helm and Burton joined another party leaving the Columbia River for Camp Floyd. They were companions more to Helm's liking—four gamblers. There were two reasons for their trip. New strikes in Montana meant rich miners, and there was the Mormon situation in Utah. The Mormons were disagreeing with the federal government—so much so that Washington sent General Johnstone to the

West with a military force to maintain order. Where there were troops there was a payroll, and where there was a payroll, there was room for a roulette wheel.

The Helm party packed one with them, along with marked cards, dice, and even a racehorse—everything, in fact, to challenge the sporting instincts of red-blooded miners and soldiers.

They left late in October—too late, as it turned out. They were confronted by deep snow and sub-zero cold in the mountain passes. Game was scarce, grub was low, and most of the party wanted to turn back. Helm persuaded them to continue, for he knew that a US marshal was behind him at the coast. In ever-deepening snow, the party struggled along. Finally, they reached the Bannock River, and the first night in camp, one of the gamblers, acting as sentry, was killed by a Native arrow.

They hastily broke camp at night and stumbled into the harsh cold and a wilderness of snow. Eventually they were forced to a standstill, horses played out, food gone. They decided to camp for the rest of the winter and live off the horses. One by one, the pack animals were killed, and as the weary weeks dragged, the five men lived on horsemeat and stray small game. Even the racehorse was sacrificed, its meat smoked in chunks. With this food, the five decided to make a final attempt to reach Fort Hall . . . or perish.

On clumsily fashioned snowshoes, they started breaking trail. Gradually the party strung out, Helm and Burton in the lead. Then Helm proposed to Burton that they abandon the others. Burton weakly agreed. The pair finally reached the Snake River and moved down it to Fort Hall. They were now trying to exist on prickly pear and tobacco plant, the only edible thing they could find. Both were practically starving, and Burton was snow-blind.

In the end, Helm decided to strike for Fort Hall alone, but when he reached it, the buildings were deserted. Returning to camp, he committed the grisliest crime so far in his depraved career. He shot Burton and cut off portions of his legs for food. Then he started for Salt Lake City. Eight miles (thirteen kilometres) along the trail he met a Native person who was also starving. He, however, wouldn't touch the human flesh.

Seven months after Helm and his party left The Dalles, the killer—who was now also a cannibal—stumbled into the camp of J.W. Powell, a fur buyer travelling to Salt Lake City. In Powell's party were James Misinger, a French-Canadian called Grande Maison, a Metis, and three Indians. The gaunt outlaw explained that his group of six had left The Dalles the previous October, had separated, and all but he and Burton had perished. He said that one night while he was collecting wood he heard a shot and found that Burton, unable to withstand the hunger and cold, had committed suicide. Later, the Native man who had encountered Helm came into Powell's camp. He knew Powell, and told the fur trader how he'd met Helm on the trail and that Helm was carrying a man's leg wrapped in a shirt.

Nevertheless, Powell took pity on Helm, equipping him with a horse, clothing, and moccasins. On the trip to Salt Lake, Grande Maison showed Powell a leather bag containing $1,400 in gold dust that Helm had asked him to keep for him. Powell returned the bag to Helm when they reached the Utah town. Undoubtedly, he had stolen it from the luckless Burton.

At Salt Lake City, Helm indulged himself with liquor and gambling, and when his gold was gone, turned to horse stealing. He joined the Johnson-Harrison gang in making forays into the Overland Mail depots. At each post was a corral holding spare horses. It was easy to catch the company men off guard and run off horses to California. Sometimes, in bolder fashion, they raided the corrals of the US Army quartermaster corps.

In 1861, Helm shot two herders guarding an army corral. A few days later, when he was in a saloon in Lodi, Utah, a soldier standing at the bar recognized him as one of the murdering horse thieves. Before the soldier could reach his army weapon, the outlaw had beaten him to the draw. The soldier slumped to the floor, a bullet through his head. Helm cowed the rest of the barroom patrons with his smoking gun as he backed out and disappeared from Lodi and southern Utah.

He next appeared in Los Angeles, a sleepy little town more Spanish than American, with a population of about five thousand. Here he robbed a storekeeper named Horne and disappeared, reappearing briefly in San Francisco, and finally reappearing at The Dalles on the Columbia.

Word came now of the Cariboo gold rush in British Columbia, and as they had during the 1858 Fraser River stampede, thousand of miners headed north. How many were murdered by Helm and other outlaws is not known, but many disappeared before they reached BC, where law and order prevailed.

Others never got a chance to leave for the new gold discovery. Take a gambler called "Dutch Fred," who plied his trade in Florence, a booming mining camp perched some eleven thousand feet (3,352 metres) in the mountains of Idaho. In the spring of 1862, the roving Helm appeared and gravitated to the leadership of a gang flourishing on the fringe of the camp.

Enmity sprang up between the outlaw and Dutch Fred, and one day Helm walked into a saloon where the gambler was playing poker. As Helm stood at the bar behind the gambler, he taunted him, hoping that Dutch Fred would draw his six-gun. Helm would then have an excuse to shoot him before he got up.

Dutch Fred, however, put his hands in the air, stood up, and leisurely walked over to Helm, who had whipped out his gun. Ignoring the weapon in the outlaw's hand, the gambler stood close to the threatening muzzle.

"If you're figuring on shooting," he said quietly, "go ahead. If not . . . get out!"

The two men eyed each other. Then Helm's features broke into a crooked sneer. The bartender, watching the pair, felt the tension lift.

"Better let me have your gun, Boone," he suggested. "I'll keep it for you."

Helm obeyed and walked out.

Half an hour later, he walked briskly into the saloon and asked for his gun; he was leaving town right away. The bartender handed it to Helm. The cannibal turned and looked toward Dutch Fred, who was still playing cards. Helm shot him in the back then slowly left the saloon.

As had happened when Helm senselessly murdered his friend Littlebury Shoot, locals were incensed at the cowardly killing of Dutch Fred. Helm knew that if citizens formed a vigilante group, he wouldn't live long. He fled again, this time to British Columbia and the Cariboo goldfields.

Just when Helm arrived is unknown, but the first reference to him being in the Cariboo is 1862, when he and a companion murdered three traders who were carrying some $30,000 in gold. This aspect of his career didn't become generally known until April 4, 1864, when a letter appeared in the *Victoria Colonist.*

While the author of the letter was not identified, he was "a gentleman who knew him [Helm] well" and went on to state "he made his way to Cariboo, where he led a life of violence which soon made the country too hot for him, and he, with some associates, killed and robbed three traders, on the trail between Antler Creek and the Forks of the Quesnelle ... "

This sketchy information was apparently all that appeared in public print until July 28, 1863. That day a letter was published in the *Toronto Mail* and on August 7 was reprinted in the *Victoria Daily Times*. Its author, A. Browning, appears to have held some sort of government position. He wrote:

In June, 1862, I was ordered to Cariboo. The year before gold had been discovered there ... I had camped at Beaver Lake ... and I met shoals of men returning from the mines. Some were dead-broke prospectors, others disappointed gamblers, and not a few who were ready for any daredevilism that would bring gold to their exchequer. One such I remember well, and the threat he uttered as I gave him good day. The trail leading down the mountain to the Forks of Quesnelle was a mile long ...

As I came near the base of the mountain I saw on the trail on the other side heading to the little village a procession of men carrying three stretchers. I found on meeting them that they were carrying three dead men. They were found on the trail coming from Cariboo, robbed and murdered, for it was known that each of them was carrying bags of gold dust from Williams' creek to the coast. Who was the murderer, or who were the murderers? Everybody said in whispers it was Boone Helm, a gambler and cutthroat who had escaped the San Francisco Vigilance Committee. He was known to have been on the trail, and he it was I probably met a few hours after the murder was committed.

There was no magistrate, nor coroner, and the solitary constable was drunk, and if he had been sober was of no use in an emergency like this. A mass meeting was called and I was elected coroner, and after the verdict of willful murder was returned I was elected magistrate, having a young Jew as magistrate's clerk. The court was formally constituted, and one or two suspicious men arrested, examined, and then let go, for everybody said the murderer was Boone Helm.

Pursuit down the trail was determined on, and $700 raised to pay the cost of pursuers. Boone, I imagine, got wind of all this, and escaped across the lines.

When I came back to the coast Mr. James Douglas told me our course was as legal as if he himself had signed my commission, and if we had caught and hung Boone Helm on proper evidence it would have been all right.

By October he had crossed to Victoria, then the second-largest community on the Pacific Coast. As he clumped along the uneven plank sidewalk with his stiff-legged horseman's gait, he thought the scene little different from Yuba City, Hangtown, or Yreka. Along Wharf Street, he noted the same "San Francisco" false fronts on the warehouses and stores, and round the corner on Lower Yates Street, the gaslit saloons seemed well patronized. From some of them came the strains of music and the laughter and squeals of the girls, and there was even the familiar Wells Fargo sign.

But there was a difference. Below the border, gunplay was common, and in many communities citizens had formed "vigilante" committees to rid themselves of thieves

Quesnelle Forks in the 1880s. The bodies of the three men Helm and his companion murdered were carried to the community.
BRITISH COLUMBIA ARCHIVES A-04045

and murderers. As Helm would learn, they hanged scores of the West's worst desperadoes. But in the colonies of Vancouver Island and British Columbia, there was official law and order. True, there were fewer than three dozen judges and policemen to uphold the law in an area larger than California, Oregon, and Washington. But the few lawmen did maintain order throughout this massive wilderness. On October 12, Helm was given a demonstration.

That day he had stolen apples from a stand and visited some saloons but refused to pay. About ten o'clock that

Sunday night, he pushed his way into the crowded Adelphi Saloon, Sam Militich, Proprietor. Helm loudly called for whisky. As was the custom, the bartender pushed a bottle and glass in front of him. After his third drink, Helm turned to go.

"You forgot something, Mister," came the quiet reminder.

Helm turned and surveyed him. "D'ye know who I am? I'm Boone Helm, and I'm a desperate character."

"I don't care who you are," came the barman's calm reply. "You owe me six bits."

Then he half inclined his head to proprietor Militich, who was standing near the door. Militich stepped outside and spotted City Police Sergeant George Blake. He beckoned the law over. "A man in here is trying to make trouble. Won't pay for his drinks."

"I think I've heard of him already tonight," was Blake's reply as he went through the swinging doors.

He eyed Helm. "All right, fellow, pay the man what you owe him."

The barroom clamour stilled, and Helm suddenly found himself the centre of interest. He liked the role, and still refused to pay.

"Then you better come with me," said the sergeant.

Helm suddenly found himself propelled through the door—not only through the door, but also down the street, to Bastion Square prison, where he was booked for disorderly conduct.

When minutes later a cell door clanged behind him, it was a new experience. For thirteen years he'd gouged, fought, shot, and stabbed his way out of one predicament after another. Gunfighter, horse thief, stage robber, cannibal, wanted for murder in half a dozen places, now he was in jail for a lousy six bits. Worse was to come.

On October 14, the *Victoria Colonist* noted:

> Suspicious Character. Boone Helm, represented as a bad character, was taken into custody on Sunday night last, upon a charge of drinking at saloons and leaving without settling his score, and for taking some apples from a stand. Sgt. Blake, who made the arrest, said that he understood the accused had killed a man at Salmon River, and fled to British Columbia. [Helm] was remanded for three days in order to see what account he can then give of himself.

On October 17, Helm appeared before Magistrate A. Pemberton, with Sergeant Blake and saloon keeper Militich ready to testify. Suddenly he realized that these people were serious.

He fell back on a plea for pity. He was a stranger, he said, friendless and without money. In fact, he said, if it hadn't been for the warm sanctuary of the prison cell the night before, he might have had to walk the streets.

Magistrate Pemberton was prepared for this ploy and asked David Ring, a local lawyer who happened to be in court, to handle the stranger's defence. Unknown to lawyer

Ring, however, his new client was in for worse trouble than either imagined. In jail, Helm had boasted of his exploits, even relating the fate of Dutch Fred in Florence, Idaho. As a consequence, Sergeant Blake told the court that he believed the prisoner to be a fugitive from Idaho, possibly wanted for murder.

The conscientious Mr. Ring objected to this statement. It was impossible under the circumstances, he told the court, for his client to get an unbiased hearing with this sort of statement being made. Nevertheless, saloon keeper Militich and Sergeant Blake gave their evidence.

Helm was convicted of disorderly conduct and ordered " . . . to find security to be of good behaviour for the term of six months . . . " The security he was ordered to find came to $450, the alternative a month in jail. Magistrate Pemberton obviously imposed the stiff penalty to give the Victoria Chief of Police, Horace Smith, time to communicate with Idaho.

Helm, unable to post the bond, was locked up and made to join the chain gang breaking rocks used for repairing Victoria's streets. In the ensuing weeks, police tried to contact the sheriff at Florence. Either he didn't exist, or the letter got lost. As a result, Helm was released at the end of the month. Three days later, word came from US authorities to hold him.

What happened from then until May is unclear, but there is a suggestion that Helm went trapping in the BC Interior with a man named Angus MacPherson and ran out of food. Only Helm returned to a Hudson's Bay Company trading post.

In his book *Vigilante Days and Ways,* Nathanial P. Langford quotes from a BC newspaper: "Upon being asked what had become of his companion, he replied with the utmost sang froid: 'Why, do you suppose that I'm a . . . fool enough to starve to death if I can help it. I ate him up, of course.'"

Langford doesn't identify which paper the account appeared in, but it wasn't the *Victoria Colonist.*

On May 1, 1863, the following news item appeared in the *Colonist:*

> A notorious character named Boon Helm, who is said to have committed a murder somewhere on the Salmon River, has been arrested by the British authorities at Fort Yale on the Fraser River, and . . . [brought] to Victoria, and lodged in our jail. The same man was once before arrested by a sergeant in our Police force and held in safe-keeping for some three or four weeks, in the expectation that a charge would be preferred against him by our cousins on the other side, and a request made for his surrender, but, as nothing transpired, he was released and three days afterwards the demand came.

News of Helm's murderous exploits had now spread, and when it was circulated in Victoria that he was departing for Olympia, there was a crowd at the wharf. It was a send-off to Helm's liking. The local press reported that he swaggered on deck, smoking a cigar, looking anything but penitent as a prisoner. From Olympia he was taken to Florence, Idaho, to stand trial for the murder of Dutch Fred.

Unfortunately for justice, the outlaw had three brothers who came west between 1848 and 1860. Little is known of them except that they all died violent deaths and the oldest was nicknamed "Old Tex." Tex was prospecting around Boise when he heard of his younger brother's trouble with the law. He went to Florence and bribed the witnesses who saw Dutch Fred getting shot in the back. As a result, the prosecution's case was weak, and Helm walked away a free man.

He then tried mining with Old Tex, but again came the old urge for travel and excitement. The US Civil War was raging, leading Tex to suggest that if Helm wanted excitement he should head south and join the Confederate Army. Off Helm went, staked by Tex to a horse, some blankets, and grub.

A week or so later, Helm stayed overnight in Virginia City, Montana, a flourishing mining community that had sprung up around an 1863 gold discovery on nearby Alder Gulch. The rich diggings yielded $30 million in the first three years and attracted some of the toughest outlaws in the Northwest.

Boss of this criminal colony was suave Henry Plummer, who had got himself elected sheriff of the community of Bannack. Plummer applied businesslike organization to its criminal operations. His gang of fifty hardened ruffians were styled "the Innocents" and split up to cover various communities.

His lieutenant, Jack Gallagher, controlled Virginia City. Under his direction were George Ives, Steve Marshland, John Wagner, Alec Carter, and "Whisky Bill" Graves. All had signed a blood oath against betrayal, and on the street they recognized each other by a knot in the handkerchief around their necks. Boone Helm was soon a member of the bloodstained brotherhood.

By 1864, the Innocents had their men everywhere, especially in mine and overland stage offices, where they could give word of gold shipments. Some were in gambling houses as dealers, tipping off the gang to the heavy winners. Available records indicate that the Innocents murdered over a hundred people from June to December of 1863 alone— over two for every member.

The robberies and killings reached such a peak by 1864 that the miners formed a vigilante committee. One day, when Henry Plummer overstepped himself, they went into action. As sheriff, he was responsible for the safety of a $14,000 shipment of gold. Plummer saw it safely on the stage, then left to meet with three confederates. Mounted, masked, and each wrapped in a blanket to avoid identification, they held up the stage and buried the gold. But fifteen-year-old Wilbur Saunders had spotted them. He took word to his aunt, for he recognized the sheriff by the red lining of his mackinaw coat.

The vigilantes grabbed the four and hanged them in Bannack. Plummer died wailing his innocence, ironically on a gallows he had had constructed. Then the vigilantes rounded up other Innocents and hanged them in twos and threes. Before long, of the fifty Innocents, about ten had fled and twenty-three had been hanged. Then came a final roundup. Some five hundred vigilantes sealed off Virginia City, and five more of Plummer's gang were caught—including Helm.

On the morning of January 14, 1864, as the sun climbed into the cloud-free sky, something more than gold held the attention of Virginia City residents. The street was clogged with people, while every rooftop and every window was jammed with spectators. Reports state that upwards of five thousand were trying to see an uncompleted log building on the main street. The owner hadn't yet installed the roof, and a wooden crossbeam connected the tops of the gable ends.

Suddenly the crowd stirred. "Here they come!" shouted an onlooker.

A lane opened in the crowd, and through it came the vigilantes and their five prisoners. When they reached the roofless building, the prisoners noticed five noosed ropes hanging from the crossbeam, underneath each rope a three-foot-high (one-metre) wooden box. John Xavier Biedler, whose brother had been murdered by one of the Innocents, stepped forward and adjusted the rope around each man's neck.

"You felt for them, didn't you?" someone remarked to him later.

"I sure did," Xavier replied. "I felt for their ears; the left one!"

The five men behind whose left ear Biedler adjusted the hangman's knot included Jack Gallagher, Plummer's lieutenant. He was over six feet (two metres) tall, broad-shouldered, wearing an army officer's cavalry greatcoat with a fur collar. His luck at the poker table was phenomenal, although anyone who did win from him was usually found dead the next day.

Another was George "Clubfoot" Lane, horse thief and stage robber. He had difficulty trying to accommodate his misshapen foot to the box's small area.

Next to him was Frank Parrish, dressed like any other miner in a dirty flannel shirt, moleskin pants, and high leather boots. Three murders had been laid at his door.

Then there was Hayes Lyons, burly and scar-faced. He had nearly escaped by climbing down the canyon walls near town. Found hiding in a shack five miles (eight kilometres) away, he admitted to two killings.

Last of the quintette was Boone Helm, described by one of the vigilantes as "the most hardened, cool, and deliberate scoundrel of the whole band." When he was arrested, he tried to elicit pity from the vigilantes, the same tactic he had used in the courtroom in Victoria. "I am as innocent as the babe unborn," he told them. " . . . I am willing to swear it on the Bible."

Among the vigilantes was newspaperman Thomas Dimsdale, who later wrote, "Anxious to see if he was so

Like these men in California, Boone Helm was hanged by a vigilante committee, a common occurrence in the US during the frontier era.
HERITAGE HOUSE

abandoned a villain as to swear this, the book was handed to him, and he, with the utmost solemnity, repeated an oath to that effect, invoking most terrific penalties on his soul, in case he was swearing falsely. He kissed the book most impressively."

The vigilantes were unimpressed. Gallagher was the first to have his box yanked away. The rope tightened and Gallagher squirmed. Helm watched his quivering body as the rope choked him and remarked, "Kick away, old fellow, I'll be in Hell with you in a minute."

Clubfoot George Lane anticipated his end by jumping off his box. One by one the Innocents died.

Finally, as Boone Helm saw his neighbour pitch to his death, he yelled, "Every man for his principles! Hurrah for Jeff Davis! Let her rip!" and leapt off his box.

The *Victoria Colonist* later carried a two-line item headed "Hanged at Last" and reading, "The notorious Boone Helm, who has so long succeeded in escaping the ends of justice, has been lynched . . . "

For two hours, the five corpses slowly revolved at the end of the five ropes strung to the single beam. Then they were buried on Cemetery Hill.

Today, Virginia City has been restored as an original link with Montana's rich mining history. Each summer tens of thousands of tourists wander through the community. The building where the five Innocents kicked their last still stands, and nearby is a row of five tombstones. The inscription on one reads: "Boone Helm hanged Jan. 14, 1864."

4

Frontier Justice on Stud Horse Creek

A FEW MONTHS AFTER BOONE HELM swung from the rafter in Virginia City, another gold rush took place in British Columbia, where his arrest in 1863 led to his eventual rendezvous with a hangman's noose. This gold rush was to a region today called East Kootenay. Here, Helm would have felt comfortable because most of the six-gun-packing miners were American, drifting north after the depletion of the California and Montana Creeks. There were saloons, gamblers, and a lawless element that Helm would have approved of, to say nothing of miners with overflowing gold pokes. But there was also an ingredient that he would have found distasteful—law and order, although it had a shaky beginning.

In 1863, gold had been found on a creek called Findlay but it proved a failure. Then, in March 1864, a group of miners discovered a new creek that proved very rich. In the vicinity they had seen a stallion, one of several thousand wild horses that roamed the area, and in its honour named the stream Stud Horse Creek. Since the nearest newspaper to record events was some hundreds of wilderness miles to the west, at New Westminster, details of the creek's early history are sketchy. In 1896, however, an article appeared in the *Fort Steele Prospector* with the following background information:

> Bob Dore recorded the first claim, calling it the Dore. Then followed the French, Fisher, Cuddy, and others. As much as $76,000 was taken out of the Dore in one day, the average being about $3,500, producing altogether in three years the sum of $521,700 . . .
>
> About 800 men wintered in the district in 1864–5. In the spring of 1865 provisions became very scarce . . . Many were forced to go out hunting and fishing to enable them to live. It was not until the middle of May that supplies arrived from the Flathead Mission. This was a very prosperous season, and there must have been from 5,000 to 8,000 men in the district. Wild (Stud) Horse creek paid better in 1865 than any creek in California did during its palmy days. Hundreds of men made $3,000 to $5,000 in a few months, and some as high as $20,000.

To part the miners from their nuggets, a ramshackle community called Fisherville appeared, named after John S.

Fisher, one of the original discoverers. Dave Griffiths, one of the few miners to spend his life in the area, wrote:

> There were about fifty buildings in the camp, including saloons, gambling houses and others . . . Everything had to be packed on horses four hundred miles, from Walla Walla. You can bet we had to pay good prices for what we got. Seventy-five cents was the flat price for everything—coffee, beans, flour—everything. I have seen flour selling in the spring of 1865 for $1.25 a pound; tobacco at $15 and they would soak it in the creek all night so it would weigh more.
>
> The money taken out in 1864 brought in about five thousand people in 1865, and that was the year that millions were taken out. I knew lots of men that cleaned up from forty to sixty thousand dollars that year. I had two partners that year, and my dividends ran one thousand to fifteen hundred dollars a week, and I would go to town every Saturday night and spend the whole thing. The next year the gold was pretty well cleaned up . . . that was the last of the rush . . .

Fisherville was also soon gone, even though it contained government offices, several cafés, stores, saloons, and a brewery. It stood on the rich Dore claim, and in 1866 was torn down and burned so that the gravel could be worked.

The arrival of Judge John Carmichael Haynes at Wild Horse Creek to deal with a shootout (see chapter 2 for details of this event) meant that British justice had arrived. The judicial show of force, however, wasn't exactly overwhelming. With Haynes was one constable, William Young, and they had been twenty days in the saddle getting there from the nearest outpost in the Okanagan. But Haynes was fortunate to have even one policeman, for there were fewer than two dozen men to maintain order in a region larger than California, Oregon, and Washington combined.

Although Haynes could not convict anyone involved in the shootout, he did try to ensure that future free-for-alls would be less deadly. He decreed that six-guns could no longer be carried. To miners from the US used to wearing one six-gun and sometimes two, as well as a bowie knife, this was a startling order. But it had worked at Victoria in 1858 when some thirty thousand heavily armed US miners arrived on their way to the Fraser River gold rush, and it worked again.

In October, government official A.N. Birch arrived at Wild Horse and reported that he found "the Mining Laws of the Colony in full force; all Customs Duties paid; no pistols to be seen, and everything as quiet and orderly as it could possibly be in the most civilized district of the Colony, much to the surprise and admiration of many who remembered the early days of the neighbouring State of California."

Despite the orderliness that so impressed Birch, there would be two more shootings on Stud Horse Creek, although by then the name had been changed to the less expressive Wild Horse Creek by a prudish government official. Despite Judge Haynes's prediction that "if there is shooting in Kootenay there will be hanging in Kootenay," those involved escaped the noose. The two murderers probably wouldn't

Pioneer judge J.C. Haynes began his career
in 1860 in the south Okanagan. HERITAGE HOUSE

have, however, had they faced a jury. As it was, in the manner
of Boone Helm, one of them met quick justice by a vigilante
committee.

For the story of one of these murderers, the notorious
thug known as One Ear Brown, see chapter 2.

The other killing on Wild Horse Creek was settled by the miners, but in less dramatic fashion. It occurred on July 4, 1868, an American holiday that the mining camp celebrated along with Canadian and British ones. By evening the camp was "well liquored up" with miners crowding into Buckly's Saloon for an Independence Day Ball, which even featured a few women. About eight o'clock an Irishman named Robert Devlin began causing a disturbance. Constable John Carrington, however, had been watching events. He came in the front door and Devlin left quickly by the back. But Carrington sensed trouble and advised Chief James Normansell.

Trouble soon came. The resentful Devlin returned to Buckly's at about nine o'clock with his revolver and indiscriminately fired four shots into the crowded saloon. Michael Walsh, a young Irishman, took the first in his shoulder. As he spun around, the second hit him in the back and killed him. The third bullet wounded Cain Mahoney, and the fourth plowed into the log wall.

Normansell and Carrington heard the shots and ran to the saloon, where they subdued Devlin. The real fight, however, threatened to be not with Devlin but with the angry miners. They quickly made their intentions clear when they looped a rope over a rafter to execute speedy justice. Fortunately for Devlin, the two policemen successfully got him to the makeshift jail. But he never came to trial.

The reason dated back to July 12, 1690. On that date the

British, under Protestant William of Orange, soundly defeated the Irish under Catholic James II at the Battle of the Boyne. Nearly two hundred years later, many Irish, including those at Wild Horse Creek, were still humiliated by the defeat.

Although Devlin had killed one Irishman and maimed another, anti-British feeling overcame a desire for law and order. Many of the Irish believed—correctly—that Devlin would be sentenced to hang or given a long jail sentence. As a consequence, one group made plans to free him. They decided that July 12, the 178th anniversary of the Battle of the Boyne, would be an appropriate date.

Some of the men who would willingly have lynched Devlin on July 4 now helped him to escape. They smuggled tools into the jail, and on the morning of July 12, after Carrington had brought him breakfast, Devlin ripped a board from the rickety cell wall and pried open the lock. He ran to a grove of trees where a horse was waiting and galloped toward the border. Although Devlin had senselessly killed one man and wounded another, when Normansell and Carrington tried to organize a posse, there was only one volunteer.

It wasn't justice, but for the Irish it was a bit of revenge for a battle they had lost nearly two centuries before. After all, they reasoned, the Wild Horse shooting had involved Irish against Irish. What right did the British have to interfere?

For Normansell and Carrington, who had saved Devlin from being lynched but who now had to report his escape, the Irishmen's reasoning was undoubtedly puzzling.

CHAPTER

5

The Wild McLean Gang

"EVERY ONE OF THE PRISONERS knew that Ussher was a constable and the killing of a constable is at all times a heinous offence. It is especially so in this country where the enforcement of the law depends entirely upon the moral effect which the power of an officer of the law has throughout the country to enforce the law's mandates . . . "

Thus did Mr. Justice Crease address the jury during the trial of Allan, Charles, and Archie McLean, and Alex Hare at New Westminster, British Columbia, in March 1880. The four had murdered Provincial Police Constable John Ussher in cold blood, wounded two other men, and used a shepherd named Kelly for target practice.

The McLeans were the mixed-race sons of Donald

The Wild McLean Gang

McLean, a Hudson's Bay Company chief trader at Kamloops who had in 1849 participated in the murder of several Native people and was himself killed by an Aboriginal person in 1864.

Allan, twenty-five, was the oldest son, physically splendid, with jet-black hair and beard. Charles was seventeen. He was tall and muscular with butting brows and, as one report noted, "a glance that was anything but frank and pleasant." Archie was fifteen, the youngest, but fairly tall for his age, with dark hair and eyes. An older stepbrother, Hector, lived nearby but was in jail at the time of the murders.

Accustomed to a wild frontier life from birth, the McLean boys lived in the saddle. They could ride as soon as they could walk, rope anything still or moving, and were excellent shots with a rifle or pistol. They spoke the French-Native patois, as well as Chinook and English.

The four outlaws began to attract attention in the fall of 1879 in the Nicola-Okanagan districts of southwestern British Columbia. They had formed a sort of gang that included Alex Hare, the seventeen-year-old son of a rancher named Nick Hare. It was common talk that person, property, and livestock were not safe when the McLeans were around.

For instance, one of the McLeans got into a fight with a Native man and bit the man's nose off. The McLean brother served a few months for this offence and came out with a yearning for vengeance. The gang robbed a Chinese man, beating him so badly over the head with a gun butt that his

Allan McLean

Charlie McLean

Archie McLean

Alexander Hare

CREDITS, CLOCKWISE: BRITISH COLUMBIA ARCHIVES A-1456, A-1458. A-1459, A-1455.

life was endangered. These wild actions were accompanied by wilder talk, since the McLeans always threatened their victims with fresh violence. Naturally, this lawlessness could not go unchecked.

Scattered throughout the Interior were officers of the BC Provincial Police. The detachment areas were vast, the population scattered, and communication difficult. The railway had not yet arrived, and stagecoaches and pack trains served the population. There was a telegraph system, though it suffered from frequent breakdowns. The provincial constable stationed at Kamloops was John Ussher. He was thirty-five, was the son of a clergyman, and had been married about eighteen months. "Johnny" Ussher, as the townspeople called him, was respected by most members of the community. He was well known to the McLeans, having arrested them for minor offences from time to time.

One day early in December 1879, rancher William Palmer, who lived about thirty-five miles (fifty-five kilometres) from Kamloops, rode in to report that his black horse had been stolen. Palmer had seen Charles McLean in possession of the animal at the foot of Long Lake. With him were his brothers, Allan and Archie, and Alex Hare. He told Ussher that he had ridden up to the four men and recognized one of them astride his black horse. As he approached, he heard the ominous click of weapons being cocked.

"Don't shoot," said Palmer. "I'm not after you."

"You hadn't better," said Allan McLean quietly. The

boys told Palmer of some trouble they had with a rancher named Moore and spoke of "bringing him to time," and, said Archie, "We'll kill any bastard who comes to arrest us."

"Why did you ride up so fast?" one of the gang asked.

"Oh, I just wanted company," said Palmer lamely and then left.

On the basis of Palmer's statement, a warrant was issued for the arrest of the McLeans on a charge of stealing Palmer's horse. Knowing that the boys acted as a gang, Constable Ussher first arrested their stepbrother, Hector. Then the officer swore in Palmer and another man named Shumway as special constables, and the trio cantered out of Kamloops on December 7 in search of the gang.

As they took the trail, Ussher told his companions that he didn't think there would be any trouble in arresting the gang. It was just after dark when they reached John McLeod's ranch. On learning their purpose, McLeod agreed to join the police party the next morning at a place called Government Camp. Soon it was apparent that they were on the right track, for at one spot in the freshly fallen snow hoof marks led deeper into a thick patch of bush. Suddenly, in a clearing, they saw four saddled horses.

"They'll never fire a shot," said Ussher. "Come on, I'll take the lead."

They had ridden but a few paces when beetle-browed Charlie McLean was noticed half-hidden behind a tree, his rifle showing. The posse reined up.

"I don't see my black horse," said Palmer.

Charlie McLean gave a sharp whistle. A shot rang out, and the bullet cut through Palmer's ice-coated beard. "That was a close one," he said, trying to control his startled horse. But the same ball had hit John McLeod. He dismounted, blood spurting from his cheeks.

Then Allan McLean was sighted taking aim from behind a tree. Palmer, armed with a shotgun, tried to get a shot at him as he dodged behind another tree. Allan fired again.

Ussher's horse, startled by the shooting, plunged and reared. Ussher slipped from the saddle. A less courageous man might have been tempted to take cover, but Ussher knew his duty, and he was a brave man. He had a revolver in his saddle holster but he left it there, perhaps thinking that his previous contact with the McLeans had earned their respect. It was a tragic misjudgment.

Ussher called on them to surrender, and then, with a deadly fusillade still going on, walked toward Alex Hare. Hare advanced, hunting knife in one hand, revolver in the other. The constable grasped the young man by the shoulder. They grappled. Hare struck repeatedly with the knife. Down went Ussher, Hare astride him. Again and again Hare used the knife, slashing Ussher in the face.

Allan McLean was heard to shout, "Kill the . . . "

Fifteen-year-old Archie darted from the shelter of a tree, revolver in hand. Holding it close to Ussher's head, he fired. Ussher lay still.

John McLeod, although hampered by the wound to his face, blasted at the outlaws with his shotgun until he was shot in the leg. As Allan McLean was loading his gun, Palmer rode in and fired at him but missed. Shumway was unarmed and could only take cover. After exchanging about thirty shots, the beaten posse rode back to Kamloops for help.

The townspeople were horrified to hear of the fate of Constable Ussher. Horses, arms, and ammunition were hastily collected, and a large body of horsemen galloped out of town to catch up with the McLeans. Arriving at the outlaws' camp just after dark, they found the campfire still burning and the body of Ussher frozen stiff. The outlaws had stripped off his coat, boots, and gloves.

In the meantime, the McLeans had ridden up to Tom Trapp's homestead some seven miles (eleven kilometres) distant. Trapp recognized them but naturally had no knowledge of the murder.

"What do you fellows want?" Trapp asked.

Charlie and Archie cocked their weapons and said they wanted firearms and ammunition. Eyeing the weapons, Trapp told them to go into the house and take what they wanted. As Allan McLean and Hare dismounted, Trapp noticed a pair of handcuffs dangling from Allan's hand. He also noticed they were bloodstained. Apprehensively, he studied the others.

"You've got blood on you," he said to one of them.

"Yes, Ussher's blood. We killed him." Charlie brandished a knife and boasted of the murder, threatening to kill anyone who came after him.

The boys were carried away with their exploit. In fact, Hare and Allan openly debated whether they would shoot Trapp there and then. But they appeared to have had second thoughts about it and rode away with Trapp yelling after them, "You'd better surrender or leave the country."

South on the wagon trail rode the outlaws. In the evening they stopped at another homestead, where a man named Roberts was killing pigs. He looked up to see four young horsemen around him and noticed they swung their rifles down. "Good evening," he said civilly. "It's a cold night."

"It sure is," answered Charlie, "and a hell of a lot of colder nights coming."

To which the youngest one added, "And a damn sight hotter times, too."

Allan and Archie dismounted and approached Robert's fire, pulling out revolvers as they asked for a man named Johnson. Apparently they had some score they wanted to settle with him.

"He's on his own place," said Roberts.

Then they asked about Canda, a local Native man who was noted for his bravery and was credited with once tangling with three bears. The gang mentioned this incident, and Allan said, "This'll be the last night he'll have to face three bears."

"He'll have to face four boys," Archie added. "I'm only fifteen, but you bet your life I'm brave."

They then told Roberts they had killed Constable Ussher. "You're fooling," Roberts replied, unbelievingly.

"You bet we killed him," said Allan.

"Here's the knife that went through him, and here's his blood on it," said Hare.

Archie held up one foot, "Here's his boots."

"And here's his coat and gloves," added Hare.

Roberts was horrified, but the McLeans had not finished. Allan drew his attention to the horses standing nearby, saying, "There's his horse, saddle, and canteen." Then he went on to describe how William Palmer had ridden in and tried to shoot him. He pointed to some shot holes in his coat and boastfully hauled Ussher's handcuffs from the saddle bag.

"Here's the handcuffs that Ussher brought to put on me—but he didn't get them on. I'll keep them for Palmer."

"Yes," broke in Charlie, "and we'll give him fifty lashes every day and fifty every night before he goes to bed." At this, Allan and Charlie laughed heartily.

They mentioned two ranchers named Ben and Sam Moore and boasted they were going to "get" them. Sickened by this talk, Roberts remarked, "I don't give a damn what you do. You can kill me if you want to."

"No, we don't want to kill you," Allan replied. "You've a large family."

Kamloops, BC, on the Thompson River, 1886. LIBRARY AND ARCHIVES CANADA

And with that the boys mounted and rode off. Next day, near Stump Lake, they spied a man named Kelly who worked as a shepherd for a settler. Kelly was sitting on a high rock.

"I'll bet I could bring him down from here," bragged Charlie McLean.

There was one report from his rifle, and the unfortunate Kelly slithered down the rock. He was dead. Hare ran forward and took a watch and chain from the body.

On they went, boasting of their exploits to workers at Thomas Scott's Ranch. Farther south at William Palmer's ranch, they forced Palmer's wife to hand over firearms and ammunition, threatening to kill anyone who barred their path.

They slept that night at a Native rancherie at the head of the Nicola River. Seeking sanctuary with the Native people was part of Allan's plan and the reason for collecting all the arms and ammunition they could find. If a posse pursued them, the gang would arm the Natives and precipitate an uprising. It would spread like bushfire, and the scattered settlements would have something more important to think about than the immediate capture of the McLeans. In any event, even if only a few Native people joined, the whole Nicola Valley would be, for the time being, at their mercy as the settlers were widely scattered and lacked arms.

Next morning the gang rode in to a Native ranch at the foot of Douglas Lake. They stabled their horses and stayed there that day and night.

In the meantime, the posse from Kamloops had increased in numbers. Homesteaders were joining the party to put an end to the lawless band. The telegraph wire to Victoria hummed with the news, and Attorney-General G.A. Walkem conferred with the superintendent of police, who hastened by schooner to Port Angeles, Washington, to alert US authorities to watch the border crossing at Colville in the Okanagan. BC lawmen, however, did not think the McLeans would cross the line, for they had fought with Native Americans and usually worsted them. On one occasion the gang had ridden into an encampment on the American side and, after stealing a number of horses, had taken one of the women and shaved her head. This was the ultimate insult, assuring the McLeans a potentially deadly reception if they ventured across the border.

The Kamloops posse, led by Justice of the Peace John Clapperton, had by now learned of the outlaws' whereabouts and converged on the cabin they occupied. They were told that a man named Thomas Richardson had parleyed with the gang through two Native men friendly to them. Richardson told the outlaws that they should surrender.

"Never!" they yelled. "Death before surrender!"

When Clapperton heard this news, he decided that no unauthorized person should meet with the outlaws. If the Natives were disposed to be friendly to the besieged boys, a general fight might ensue. Clapperton sent word to Chief Shillitnetza to stop all communication between his people and the McLeans. The chief co-operated fully, telling the white men "to shoot any Indian found going or coming from the McLean cabin."

Clapperton was a shrewd frontiersman—he wanted the killers out of the cabin with the least bloodshed. He knew that they had neither food nor water and must eventually give up or commit suicide. He split the posse into three shifts so that there was a constant watch. "Shillitnetza" was the password.

Morning came with no sign of life from the small cabin, though later in the day Clapperton detected through field glasses signs that thirst was troubling the boys. They had torn up the cabin's floor to reinforce the walls, and through a chink in the logs near the ground could be seen attempting to scrape in a little snow. Rifle bullets from the posse smashing into the logs quickly stopped the attempt. Then they tried poking straws through to suck up any moisture. Apart from this activity, the day passed uneventfully. On December 11, a second party of settlers arrived under the leadership of another Justice of the Peace named Edwards.

Then Clapperton asked Chief Shillitnetza if his son, Saliesta, would take a message to the McLeans under cover of a white flag. The Native boy agreed, and Clapperton wrote out the following message:

> McLean Bros, and Alex Hare: Will you surrender quietly? If so, send in your arms and I guarantee your personal safety. No surrender, and we burn the house over your heads.
>
> Jn. Clapperton, JP

The Native messenger was sent in with paper and pencil for a reply. Saliesta reined in his horse about three hundred feet (ninety metres) from the cabin and waved his signal of truce. Finally, through a crack in the cabin door, a tiny piece of rag fluttered for a moment in the raw December air. Saliesta moved to within speaking distance. More minutes passed. He advanced to the door and was handed a paper. Bending low in the saddle, Saliesta galloped back to the watching ranchers.

On the scrap of paper, Clapperton read:

Mr. Clapperton,
Sir:—
The boys say that they will not surrender, and so you can burn the house a thousand times over.
Alexr. J. Hare.

I wish to know what you all have against me. If you have anything, please let me know what it is.
A.H.

Clapperton decided to carry out his threat and burn the cabin. Large bundles of hay were dragged into position and saturated with coal oil, but they were wet and refused to burn. For two hours they tried—two hours fraught with danger, for the McLeans kept up a desultory fire all the time. In his report on the siege Clapperton noted, "The bullets shot at the bales passed through with deadly force so that the breastwork was useless."

The leader of the posse decided to try another attempt at parley. A man named John Leimard offered to carry the flag this time. He was told to advance and wave it, and if an answering signal was shown, to return for instructions. The signal was given and answered, and a settler said he would carry on the parley. He reported that hunger and thirst were doing their work and that the boys were in bad shape. He returned to the cabin with pencil and paper, and the outlaws laboriously wrote, "We will surrender if not ironed and supplied with horses to go to Kamloops."

A message was sent back: "Surrender by coming outside and laying down your arms. We will protect you."

Grim-faced ranchers with cocked rifles expectantly viewed the little log structure. Then the cabin door slowly opened, and one by one the outlaws appeared. They discharged their firearms in the air and then threw them on the ground. In this act, they displayed their Native ancestry: it was common practice when Native people surrendered for them to fire off unused ammunition.

Tired and drawn, their tongues swollen from thirst, the McLean gang staggered forward, hands aloft. Their six revolvers, five rifles, and two shotguns were quickly gathered up, and they were handcuffed and placed in a wagon for Kamloops. In the cabin, searchers found John Kelly's watch and chain.

Thanks to the cool and cautious conduct of the two posse leaders, Clapperton and Edwards, the McLean-Hare gang had been captured with but one casualty. A man whose horse had strayed too near the cabin was shot in the chest when he ran forward to retrieve the animal. Fortunately, it was only a flesh wound.

At Kamloops, the four were committed for trial on charges of murder. Hare made a partial confession, and intimated that the gang had expected aid from the Nicola Native bands.

The prisoners were taken to New Westminster and locked up on Christmas Day 1879.

At New Westminster, a special assize opened on March 13, 1880, at which the McLeans and Hare faced the bar of justice. Hector McLean, the oldest brother, charged with aiding and abetting, was held in jail to be dealt with later.

Witnesses for the Crown were examined and cross-examined, and at the end of five days, Mr. Justice Crease charged the jury in a two-hour speech remarkable for its clarity and force. He complimented the settlers of the Kamloops area for their adherence to the principles of British justice, implying that on other soil the McLeans would probably have been lynched.

The jury was out for twenty-two minutes and returned with a verdict of guilty. Justice Crease then sentenced them to death. On hearing the sentence, Hare remarked, "It's a well deserved sentence, your Lordship."

The prisoners shambled out of court, their heavy old-fashioned leg irons held to the waist by a leather thong. When Allan, who was manacled to Archie, passed William Palmer, he viciously kicked him in the leg. The constable in charge struck Allan with a cane, and Archie lashed out at the constable before being hustled to the cells. They continued to be troublesome prisoners, and there were repeated attempts at escape, in addition to bursts of disorderly conduct.

The McLeans did not hesitate to appeal their sentence on the grounds that as no commission had been issued, there was no assize, and therefore no trial. The Supreme Court of British Columbia agreed with them, and on June 27, 1880, ruled that the prisoners had been illegally tried. They were to remain in custody until discharged by due course of law.

At Kamloops, in October, Hector McLean was acquitted of the charge of being an accessory before the fact. A month later, Allan, Charles, and Archie McLean, with their accomplice, Hare, were once more placed on trial in New Westminster for the murder of Ussher and Kelly.

Again, the jury found them guilty. The second trial had only served to delay their execution. In confinement they became more unruly than ever and had to be chained to the walls of their cells for days at a time. On one occasion, Archie threatened the warden with an iron bucket, and on another, a knife was found in Allan's blankets. On one routine examination, prison officers discovered that his irons were partially filed through with a file suspected to be from another prisoner.

Then one day a mixed-race man named John Henry Makai, who was serving a short sentence on a liquor charge, asked the warden if he could act as executioner for the McLeans. Puzzled by this odd request, the warden told Makai that an official executioner would be used. However, he kept Makai under observation and later learned that the McLean gang had made a compact with him. If Makai was appointed executioner, he would secretly cut through the execution ropes, and when the trap was sprung, the outlaws would drop unharmed—the few uncut threads breaking under the strain. They would then whip out knives and cut their way to freedom. Makai, on release, was to be rewarded with a hundred head of cattle and forty horses, which he would collect from Hector in Kamloops.

For the McLeans, however, there would be no escape. On January 28, 1881, the New Westminster *Mainland Guardian* carried the following news item:

> A SINISTER DISPLAY—As we passed the gate of our city gaol yesterday morning, we observed the pieces of timber all cut and shaped in readiness to be put together to form the scaffold on which the McLeans and Hare are to suffer death on Monday morning next. It is bad enough that their minds are now dwelling on their approaching end, but to have their ears assailed with the tap, tap, tap of the hammers that nail together the "fatal gallows tree'" is something terrible to endure . . .

The hanging went as scheduled on January 31, with the paper carrying the following account:

> Monday morning dawned cold, sharp, and clear. At 7:30 quite a group of our leading citizens had gathered within the four walls of the city prison (including the scaffold contractors) Messrs. Fry & Calback . . .
>
> The condemned men were early attended by their spiritual advisors, Revd. Father Horris and two other priests. After partaking of a light breakfast, devotions were resumed, and the utmost penitance and contribution was displayed by the four culprits. A little before 8 a.m., the executioner proceeded to pinion them by means of stout leather straps: the hands were fastened in front, and a strap passing above

the elbows behind. Shortly after, the procession was formed in the following manner:—The Executioner in front, Sheriff Morrison and Prison Surgeon Trew, Chief of Police and Warden of the Gaol, Father Horris and Assistant Priests, Allan and Archie, with a Policeman on each side, Charley and Hare, with Constable on each side; they proceeded to the place of execution, where all eyes were fixed on the unfortunate men; as they passed along, they said "good-bye" to those near them, and mounted the scaffold in pairs. Hare stood at the West end, Charlie and Allan in the center, Hare was the first to speak; he said: "I forgive every one and thank everyone for their kindness; I am guilty of the crimes laid to my charge, and justly deserve the impending punishment." Charlie spoke next, in the same strain; his pale ashy lips and unsteady motion might have arisen from cold or from the strongly betrayed emotions within. Allan hoped all young men would take a warning by his sad position, and faltered words of thanks to all; he asked forgiveness for his crime, and said he was prepared to enter the unseen and unknown world beyond the grave. Archie followed in the same words almost, which were repeated by the Revd. Father to those in front of the gibbet. The Hangman then adjusted the ropes, commencing with Hare; the signal was given by the Sheriff, and in an instant the doomed men fell. Death appeared to have been almost instantaneous; with the exception of Charlie, who showed slight convulsions, they scarcely moved a muscle. After hanging the usual time, the bodies were cut down and decently interred. After the drop fell, something like a sigh of relief escaped from the spectators, who felt that innocent blood had been avenged, and the law vindicated.

6

Yukon's Christmas Day Assassins

WITH A FAT CANADA GOOSE sizzling in the oven, Corporal Patrick Ryan of the NWMP's Hootchikoo Detachment jerked open the door for the third time that Christmas night. He gazed impatiently across the moon-drenched surface of the Yukon River but failed to see any dark figure moving against the violet-tinted snowdrifts. He had invited telegraph lineman Ole Olsen to share his Christmas dinner, but there was no sign of him. "Guess he's run into a bunch at Fussell's roadhouse and the boys are whooping it up," he thought as he closed the door. But still he wondered. Ole Olsen wasn't the type of person to casually break a promise.

It was the closing week of 1899. At Dawson City, fifty

miles (eighty kilometres) to the north, miners were fighting the frozen creeks in their search for gold—creeks that since the Klondike stampede of 1898 had already yielded gold by the hundreds of tons. While most of the fifty thousand or so men who had trekked north the previous year were honest, a few came to mine not the gravel but those who had wrested the gold from its frozen bed.

To help protect the miners who had struck pay gravel and then ventured along the four-hundred-mile (six hundred and forty-kilometre) wilderness trail to Skagway, where boats connected to Vancouver and Seattle, NWMP Superintendent Sam Steele had increased the strength of the force in Yukon. Now ten officers and over two hundred and thirty scarlet-coated men patrolled the silent reaches, their duties ranging from collecting customs dues to slashing trails, to controlling the honky-tonks in Dawson City, to protecting miners from the criminal element. To further ensure the safety of those travelling through the frozen wilderness, the resourceful Sam Steele had scattered detachments along the route.

There was Fort Selkirk, 170 miles (275 kilometres) south of Dawson; then Minto, 18 miles (29 kilometres) farther on; Hootchikoo, 16 miles (26 kilometres) beyond; and, at an equal distance, Five Fingers; and so the chain of police posts continued right to the Alaska border. It made miners packing thousands of dollars of yellow gold dust feel safer to realize that the trail was under the vigilance of these Mounted Police. Without them, they would be entirely at the mercy of the human vultures who, despite all attempts to keep them out, had found their way into the gold camps.

As a further means of keeping in closer touch, the Mounted Police had just completed a frontier telegraph line between Dawson and the Alaska boundary. It was a rough affair, strung from tree to tree, and Ole Olsen and his fellow linemen were kept busy freeing the line of fallen trees and other debris that encumbered it after every thaw or blizzard.

Ole never did appear at Corporal Ryan's that Christmas Day. By December 31, he was still missing, and Ryan was getting anxious. Restlessly, he again glanced over a report he had received from Constable Alexander Pennycuick of Fort Selkirk Detachment. It referred to two undesirables named Tom Miller and Charlie Ross who had robbed an ice-locked scow at Hell's Gates and were said to be hiking southward.

Well, it was a cinch they hadn't passed through Hootchikoo, or he would have seen them. They must still be somewhere between Hootchikoo and Fort Selkirk. All he could do was watch for them. Then his thoughts swung to the missing lineman. Had Ole met with an accident, or had the Christmas thaw given him extra work? Corporal Ryan decided to investigate.

Slipping on his parka and worming his moccasined feet into snowshoe thongs, he crunched over the crusted drifts toward Minto, eyes alert. The Christmas thaw and subsequent bitter cold had crusted the snow, but there had since been another storm.

Corporal Patrick Ryan waited for a Christmas guest who never arrived. LIBRARY AND ARCHIVES CANADA

At a point where a cut-off known as the Pork Trail led through the woods, he hesitated. The Pork Trail had been slashed by freighters hauling supplies to Dawson to avoid a wide bend in the river, and the telegraph line followed it. Ryan decided to take it, hoping to find some clue to Ole's inexplicable absence. He had covered some nine miles (fourteen kilometres) when a slight depression, running at right angles to the trail, caught his eye. It might have been an animal path but looked much more like a snowed-in trail made by human feet. He decided to investigate.

For twenty minutes, he walked parallel with the depression, careful not to disturb it, and then suddenly stopped. Before him an abandoned tent arose from a wall of unbarked logs. The absence of animal stretchers told him that it was not a trapper's camp. Why, then, a tent so far from the beaten track? His eyes took a swift inventory as he stepped in. The bunk was large enough for two men. Suddenly he tensed. Piled in a corner were sacks and boxes of provisions, each bearing the mark of the trading company whose goods had been pilfered from the scow at Hell's Gates. He had stumbled on Miller and Ross's hangout! He quickly listed the contents of the tent. Then, stepping out into the snow, he made his way thoughtfully back toward the Pork Trail.

Darkness had settled upon the woods when he at last reached the long ebony rectangle of Captain Fussell's roadhouse, broken by orange squares of light that shone cheerily on the purple drifts. From the stovepipe, a white column of vapour rose into the bejewelled sky. From the ice on his parka, Ryan realized it must be nearly -60°F (-50°C).

Throwing open the door, he entered and shook hands with Captain Fussell. Dropping into a babiche-netted chair before the red-hot box-stove, he listened to the captain's account of the latest upriver gossip.

"Say, Fussell," Ryan eyed the tall, rawboned figure anxiously, "what happened to Ole Olsen? He was due at my place for dinner on Christmas Day, but hasn't shown up yet."

"What!" Fussell's jaw sagged. "That's damned queer. Ole left here early Christmas morning. Couldn't keep him. Said you'd be waiting with dinner for him."

Ryan frowned. "Was he alone?"

"No. Two men from Dawson bunked here the night afore. Fred Clayson, a fellow from Seattle who'd struck it rich on the creeks, and another guy named Lynn Relfe, a caller in one of the dance halls. They were on their way outside with quite a pile. Figgered on spendin' Christmas here only Ole was so anxious to keep that date with you, they decided to pull out with him. Don't tell me you didn't see them!"

"Neither one of them. Think I'll hike back to Five Fingers in the morning. Maybe Sergeant Parker'll know something. Give me a sheet of paper, I want to drop a line to Alex Pennycuick at Fort Selkirk. Guess you can find someone to take it over."

Late the following evening, Ryan shook off his snowshoes, entered the low log barracks at Five Fingers and clasped the sinewy hand of Sergeant Parker. Through the frosty air boomed the menacing roar of the nearby rapids, mingling with the companionable crackling of the red-hot stove. Ryan gazed anxiously about the white-painted living room for a sign of the missing Olsen; a glance that wasn't lost on Parker.

"Well, Corporal, what's eating you?" he asked.

"Have you seen Olsen? He left Fussell's early Christmas

morning for my place and seems to have disappeared. Figured he might be here."

"Haven't seen him since the twenty-first," Parker answered with obvious surprise. "Constable Buxton came back on the twenty-fourth with all Olsen's tools except his pliers and file. Fact is, Ryan, I've been worried myself. It was pretty soft on Christmas Day, and I've a hunch he hit a bad spot and went through. This Yukon's treacherous. Solid ice one day, shell ice the next. All depending on the current. Too bad if he got drowned."

Ryan's eyes narrowed. "But don't forget, he was travelling with Relfe and Clayson and . . . between them they were packing a tidy amount of coin. Guess I'll have a bite and hit the hay. I'm meeting Pennycuick on the Pork Trail at noon tomorrow."

With growing apprehension, Ryan returned to his detachment at Hootchikoo the next morning and continued until he came to the Pork Trail. Fresh tracks showed that Pennycuick was there ahead of him. Then, through the frost-rimmed willows, he espied the tall angular form of the Englishman near the tent.

"Hello, Ryan," he laughed, "I've just been poking around this tent you found. It's Miller and Ross's hideout all right. Here—look at these draft holes," he said, pointing to the stovepipe. "They form a perfect figure eight. Saw those same pipes and stove in Miller's camp at Hell's Gates on December eleventh. Three days later, when I returned with a warrant, they'd vamoosed. Here's something else I found." On a rough spruce table were a 40.82 rifle, a bag of cartridges, a pair of pliers, and a file.

"Pennycuick," announced Ryan grimly, "those pliers belong to Ole. We've got more than a scow robbery on our hands. This looks like murder."

That night, word of the discovery was flashed to Dawson and Tagish. The whole force promptly snapped into action. Alert eyes scrutinized every traveller mushing along the icy trail toward the Alaska boundary for men answering the description of Miller and his partner.

The following day, Staff Sergeant George M. Graham was gazing through the frosted windows of the Tagish barracks, near the Alaska boundary, at the most stupid piece of fool-hardiness he had witnessed in many a day. A fur-coated man in a sled was whipping a team of black horses furiously across the river toward an area where the swift current undercut the ice. The driver had swerved aside from the regular trail, which passed the barracks, and was making directly for the dangerous ice. Behind him loped a magnificent St. Bernard.

"There's one bird who doesn't place much value on his hide," Graham said to Constable Thomas A. Dickson, who was writing at a nearby table. "Better slip over to the stable and grab a rope—we're going to need it in a minute. Look how that ice is sagging! There! I told you. One of his horses is through. Come on. Quick."

Plowing through the loose snow, they saw that one horse

was partly submerged, while the other animal was thrashing frenziedly about. The driver, a heavy-set, beetle-browed man, was flailing the fear-maddened animals mercilessly with his whip.

Snatching the whip from the driver's hand, Graham swept him angrily aside. "What's the big idea, abusing these beasts?" he shouted. "Here, grab this rope and help get 'em on good ice."

They got the team onto safe ice and then to the barracks. Here Graham turned furiously on the big man. "What in hell possessed you to drive into that mess? Any cheechako would know better. What's your name anyway?"

"George O'Brien," he mumbled gruffly.

Graham eyed him coldly. This O'Brien had shown a suspicious anxiety to avoid contact with the police. A swift, appraising glance had already shown a police robe on the sled. How had it come into his possession? Police equipment wasn't bartered about the country.

While O'Brien changed his wet clothes, Graham questioned him about the robe. Shifty-eyed and sullen, O'Brien explained that he'd obtained it from the officer commanding at Dawson some time before. Then, attired once more in dry clothing, O'Brien sought the entertainment afforded by the notorious Native woman Jenny in her cabin not far away.

Graham thoughtfully watched the stocky figure disappear in a world of spinning flakes, then scribbled a telegram to Inspector William Scarth at Dawson.

THE LAW AND THE LAWLESS

A few hours later he received a reply. O'Brien's story was correct. Disgustedly, he tossed the wire to Dickson. "Guess we can pass O'Brien up. Thought we'd landed a suspect, but Dawson says his story about the robe's okay."

Shortly afterward, however, the operator entered with another telegram. It caused the sergeant to smile and sent him plowing through the storm. Entering Jenny's squalid cabin, he met the steely challenge in the eyes of the half-drunken O'Brien.

"O'Brien, alias Tom Miller," he snapped, "I arrest you for that scow robbery at Hell's Gates last December. Throw on your coat. And what happened to Graves—that partner of yours who's been calling himself Ross? Did time with you in Dawson."

"Miller!" O'Brien laughed hoarsely. "Who in hell's Miller? My name's O'Brien. I don't know nothing about your scow."

While O'Brien cursed in the guardhouse, Graham and Dickson searched his sled. It contained a .30-30 Winchester, a supply of ammunition, two revolvers, two empty shells for a .41 Winchester revolver, and a telescope. On the floor was a dark stain that might have been made by animal or human blood.

As he reread the last telegram from Dawson, Graham chuckled. So closely had his description of O'Brien matched Miller's as given in Pennycuick's report, that Inspector Scarth had had second thoughts and wired

Graham to charge him with the scow theft. A hurried check had disclosed that O'Brien and a man named Graves had been released from Dawson jail that fall. O'Brien, destitute of funds, had been given sufficient rations to take him out of town.

Graham pondered. How, then, had he secured sufficient money since to buy a good team and all the other equipment? The sergeant flashed another wire to Dawson. Scarth replied that he was hurrying south by dog team, bringing with him Harry Maguire, a former Pinkerton detective.

Meanwhile, Pennycuick was continuing his investigations in the vicinity of the Pork Trail. Somewhere in the area, he felt convinced, lay the answer to the mystery of the missing men. Quiet and unassuming, Pennycuick believed in employing what he termed common sense. And that common sense told him that the Christmas thaw would, as a result of the subsequent cold snap and crusting snow, leave a permanent record of what had happened that day. All he had to do was find the place of the crime and remove the new snow.

A careful survey disclosed signs of someone having climbed the sloping bank at the point where the tent trail reached the river. Then he noticed something that had previously escaped him. From the river to the tent, branches had been lopped from trees and some chopped down. But why? Certainly not to clear the trail, for they were cut an arm's length overhead.

Turning, Pennycuick gazed southward through the slashed bush from a hillock behind the tent. It provided a perfect view of some ten miles (sixteen kilometres) of the frozen Yukon! Now he understood the significance of that telescope found on O'Brien's sled. From this hidden tent, a man with a telescope could watch, unseen, anyone following the river trail. To Pennycuick, the discovery was alarming.

Leaving the knoll, he examined some of the fallen trees. Each had been cut with an axe that had three distinct notches in the blade. Following the tent trail back to the riverbank, Pennycuick swept away the loose snow with some spruce boughs, disclosing a furrow in the crusted snow that could have been made by dragging a body over it while the snow was melting. It led to a hole in the ice, which had frozen over. He picked up a tuft of yellow hair that might have belonged to O'Brien's St. Bernard and slipped it in his pocket. Then, following the furrow to the top of the bank, he found himself standing in a small snow-covered clearing ringed with frosted bushes.

Had Clayson, Relfe, and Olsen, he wondered, as they swung southward that balmy Christmas morning, been enticed from the river and ambushed near this spot? He confided his suspicions to Detective Maguire, who had replaced Corporal Ryan, then hurried to Fort Selkirk to confer with Inspector Scarth.

Scarth was worried and anxious. George O'Brien,

arrogant and angry, was demanding his release. Not a shred of direct evidence had been produced to justify him being confined. And now the moccasin telegraph had brought word that Clayson and Olsen had followed a rush to a new gold strike on the Big Salmon and were working claims. It looked very much as though the police case was going to disintegrate. O'Brien could not be held indefinitely without direct evidence to connect him with either the robbery or the murder.

When Pennycuick and Maguire returned to the cut-off on the Pork Trail, they brought along O'Brien's big St. Bernard. Unleashing the animal a short distance from the tent trail, Pennycuick put an experiment into effect.

"Go home!" he ordered. The St. Bernard wagged his tail, gazed questioningly at him, then lay down on the snow. "Go home!" Again Pennycuick repeated his command.

Slowly the dog arose, surveyed him for a moment, then trotted off. At the junction of the trails, he swung north toward the tent. Half an hour later they found him snuggled within, obviously at home!

Maguire laughed understandingly. "Well, Pennycuick, if that doesn't tell its own story I'll eat my hat. O'Brien's up to his neck in this. It's just a case of rounding up evidence. I don't believe Clayson and Olsen were ever near the Big Salmon. Come along and I'll show you why."

Through the snow-covered spruce they crunched south-ward to the opening in the woods that Pennycuick had thought a likely place for an ambush. For a considerable distance around, Maguire had painstakingly removed the soft snow down to the glazed surface.

Clutching the constable's arm, he pointed to where two dark red splotches stained the snow's surface. Some distance away were four more ominous stains. Frozen pools of blood!

Pennycuick nodded. "Just as I thought. Those men were seen from the tent, lured into an ambush, and murdered. Then their bodies were dragged to the river and shoved through the ice. Guess the killers figured they'd be carried down to the sea, or crushed to pieces at breakup. Still— we've got to get evidence to satisfy a jury, and Yukon juries are hard-boiled. Let's give this clearing the once-over, and then we'll examine the snow around the tent."

Day after day, in the biting cold of –50°F (–45.6°C), they searched. On hands and knees, they sifted the freezing snow through icy fingers. Gradually, painstakingly, evidence unfolded. A careful examination of every tree disclosed bullet-scarred bark and clipped-off branches. With Maguire's help, Pennycuick calculated the angles of trajectory and the points from which the shooting had been done. To the mounting pile of evidence were added some splinters of bone, human hair, a 40.82 shell, a watch that had stopped at 9.02, part of a tooth broken from the root, and part of another gold-filled tooth smeared with the lead of a bullet.

At last they moved back to the tent. Standing at the

doorway, Pennycuick surveyed the unbroken surface of the snow.

"Mac, if you'd done away with anyone, and wished to get rid of incriminating articles you couldn't burn, what would you do?"

Maguire thought for a moment. "I'd throw 'em away— scatter 'em about."

"Exactly!" Thrusting his hand into his pocket, Pennycuick produced a few coins, a pocket knife, and a key. With quick jerks, he sent them spinning across the snow. Then, with a stick, he marked a semicircle outside the farthest point where they had dropped and picked up the broom. "Come on, Mac, we'll sweep up all the loose snow inside this line and sift it."

Again they went to work. The results surpassed the constable's expectations. First they discovered a lineman's leather belt, then a key, an axe with three notches in the blade that corresponded with the cuttings on the trees, a peculiar coin that Relfe was known to have carried as a charm, and, finally, the charred embers of a fire. Among the ashes were remnants of burned clothing, some buttons bearing the name of a Seattle clothier, and eyelets from a pair of factory-made moccasins. Finally, from a shovelful of soft snow Pennycuick withdrew a ragged scrap of paper and whistled softly. It was Ole Olsen's receipt from Fussell's roadhouse for breakfast— and it was dated Christmas morning!

Unfortunately, the most necessary evidence for a murder trial was still lacking. Despite the fact that Scarth had sent parties to cut and dynamite the river ice and drag the bottom, no bodies had been found. O'Brien, resolute and angry, was demanding his release.

At last, with a thunderous roar, the Yukon River cast aside its icy fetters. Millions of tons of ice reared and leapt and went toward the sea. There seemed little hope of finding any frail human bodies after that massive force had expended itself. Nevertheless, Mounted Police patrols pushed out in canoes and commenced a systematic search of sloughs and sandbars.

On May 30, the citizens of Dawson were electrified by the news that a bullet-ridden body, identified as Clayson's, had been found on a sandbar near Fort Selkirk.

On June 11, another body was found floating downriver. In the vest pocket were visiting cards bearing the name Lynn Relfe. Sixteen days later, the territory was brought to a still higher pitch of tension by the discovery of Ole Olsen's body on a sandbar. Each body was riddled with three or four bullets, proving that the shooting had been wild. Olsen's skull had been crushed in. The bodies were shipped to Dawson, where it was found that the two broken teeth discovered near the tent trail exactly fitted roots in the gums of Relfe and Clayson.

On the sweltering day of June 10 nearly a year later, O'Brien's trial opened in the log courthouse at Dawson City. From the dock, the prisoner, self-possessed and aggressive, glowered at the crowd of miners, gamblers, and flashy women

Fred Clayson was one of three men whom George O'Brien helped to murder. LIBRARY AND ARCHIVES CANADA

from the honky-tonks. Grimly, a jury of miners and merchants awaited the testimony of eighty witnesses it had taken many months to assemble from all parts of the continent. Upon a table were piled exhibits that almost exhausted the alphabet, including tree stumps showing three notches, the notched axe itself, analysts' reports on the stains found in the snow and on the floor of O'Brien's sled, two broken teeth smeared with the lead of bullets, and a key found near the tent, which had been found to fit Clayson's safe in Seattle.

Slowly the story unfolded. O'Brien and Graves had met in the Dawson jail. O'Brien had first propositioned a fellow convict named Williams, then another named Sutton, with the suggestion that when released, they camp at some isolated spot, watch for gold-burdened miners, rob and kill them, and push their bodies through the ice. The swift current of the Yukon would do the rest. Both had received the proposition coldly, but Graves had succumbed to the hypnotism of O'Brien's wily tongue.

When the prisoners' time had been served, the police had furnished them with an axe, a stove, and some provisions. On December 12, O'Brien and Graves had stopped at Fussell's roadhouse. Four days later, O'Brien had stood guard while Graves carried their purloined supplies from the Arctic Express Company's ice-locked scow into the bush; then both had disappeared. On December 26, Fussell had observed smoke rising in silvery clouds above the treetops in the area where the tent was subsequently located—and wondered. Next day, O'Brien had emerged unexpectedly from the willows fringing the Pork Trail and followed a Mr. and Mrs. Prater south along the river trail toward Tagish. One night, he'd been seen counting a large roll of greenbacks. On another night, he'd displayed a peculiar gold nugget—the corners bent over almost like fingers clasping a small nugget within—that had formerly belonged to Relfe.

Breathlessly, the jury and spectators listened as Pennycuick and Maguire filled in the details of what had happened on that tragic Christmas Day.

Between December 17 and 24, Graves and O'Brien had packed the stolen supplies to their rendezvous in the woods, cleared an aisle through the forest with the notched axe, and prepared the death trap. Through the telescope, they'd watched three travellers moving southward on Christmas morning. They'd hurried down the tent trail and prepared their ambush. Below the bank, they could hear the men talking and laughing as they swung along.

Suddenly, Graves had appeared on the ice with his 40.82. Frightened, the men scrambled up the bank and dug for cover, only to be met with a fusillade of shots from O'Brien's .30-30. Confused by the unexpectedness of the attack, the three travellers then milled around. O'Brien and Graves were shooting wildly. Clayson dropped sixteen feet (almost five metres) from the bank. Lynn Relfe sprang for cover; a bullet tore through his cheek, clipping out a gold-filled tooth; another found his brain. Olsen, wounded, struggled for the woods, only to be overtaken and bludgeoned to death.

Coats were stripped from the bodies and thoroughly searched. A hole was cut in the ice, and the victims consigned to the chilly clutches of the Yukon. Having obliterated, as they thought, all signs of the struggle, O'Brien and Graves then kindled a fire outside the tent and attempted to destroy the remaining evidence.

Prosecuting Attorney F.C. Wade, Q.C., wove one piece of evidence into another, cementing them with the exhibits. On the ninth day of the trial, O'Brien, stolid up to this time, gazed with lowering face about him. Sergeant Graham testified to finding two bills sewn into the soles of O'Brien's boots and an additional $2,000 secreted between the runners and the iron shoeing of the sled taken from him at Tagish.

In a brilliant defence, O'Brien's lawyer attempted to sweep aside the evidence as purely circumstantial. Something more than flimsy allegations was necessary when a man's life was at stake, he thundered. Wade rose to his feet.

"Your Honour, permit me to produce Quartermaster–Sergeant Telford."

When the red-coated sergeant entered the witness box, the prosecuting attorney passed the notched axe over. "Sergeant, do you recognize this axe?"

"Yes, sir. When O'Brien's time was up, I returned his

sled, dog, tent, and revolver, but couldn't find an axe, so I gave him this one with a sort of apology for the three nicks. I'd know it anywhere."

The last witness, extradited from Seattle where he had been serving a term of imprisonment, was known as the "Clear Kid" around the Dawson dance halls, his actual name being West.

In a peculiar medley of Bowery jargon and Northern slang, ex-faro dealer West told of occupying the cell behind O'Brien the previous winter and of being approached by him to kill and rob passing miners "to clean up a bunch o' coin" and then to "chuck their bodies in the drink." Preferring petty larceny to murder, he'd refused, gone his own way, and promptly landed in jail again.

At dawn on the morning of August 23, 1901, O'Brien mounted the scaffold in the barracks yard at Dawson City. Swaggering and unrepentant, he dropped to his doom.

Graves, alias Ross, was never seen again. But late that summer, a decomposed and bullet-riddled body was found on a sandbar far down the Yukon River. After the murders, O'Brien had obviously shot his partner and pushed him through the ice to dispose of the only living testimony to his guilt. Unfortunately, in his murderous planning, he had failed to include Detective Maguire, Constable Pennycuick, and the other red-coated policemen who had so brilliantly amassed the evidence that led O'Brien to the gallows.

7

The Saga of Simon Gun-an-Noot

IN WESTERN CANADA'S HISTORY, MANY a colourful character with a gun in his hand and a price on his head has taken to the wide-open spaces. If an outlaw's vivid career has ended on a slab or in a cell, for a brief time he is something of a celebrity. Of these fugitives, a bare handful have become a sort of legend. These few include men like Bill Miner (see *Bill Miner . . . Stagecoach & Train Robber*, Heritage House), and that most famous of all Aboriginal outlaws, Simon Gun-an-Noot. He is famous because, after dodging police for an unbelievable thirteen years, he surrendered and was found innocent of the murder charge that originally made him an outlaw.

Gun-an-Noot was a full-blooded Kispiox, his home at

Hagwilget, close to Hazelton in the mountains of north-western British Columbia. He was an impressive man, big for a Native man, and not only proud and erect, but with muscles and sinews as tough as whipcord—the result of years of backpacking and canoeing. His very appearance hinted at his reputation as a successful hunter and trapper, and among whites he was known as a truthful and fair-dealing man. He converted to Christianity early in his youth, always proudly wearing his church medallion on feast days. Simon Gun-an-Noot was devoted to his young wife, Sarah.

The saga of Gun-an-Noot began in June 1906, when he came out of the wilderness to sell his fur to the Hudson's Bay post at Hazelton. After squaring up his jawbone (credit), he left for home at Kispiox and that evening joined in a home-coming celebration at a nearby roadhouse at Two Mile.

While Gun-an-Noot wasn't exactly a drinking man, he did his share. Around midnight, things got a bit noisy at the roadhouse and a miner called Alec Mcintosh made some derogatory remarks about Native people in general, and the morality of Kispiox women in particular.

"Does that include my wife?" snapped Gun-an-Noot as he seized a couple of fistfuls of Mcintosh's shirt and pulled the miner within inches of his face.

"Yes, your wife, too!" sneered Mcintosh in his half-drunken abandon. Gun-an-Noot's rock-hard fist cut off further comment, and with Mcintosh flat on the floor, he departed.

Around dawn the next day, a party of Babine Native

111

people walking the trail to Hagwilget found their path barred by a man sprawled on his back, dead. Hurrying to Hazelton, they told Johnny Boyd of their discovery. He in turn passed on the information to Constable Jim Kirby of the Provincial Police. Shortly afterward, Kirby and the local coroner, Edward H. Hicks-Beach, were on the scene. The dead man was Alec Mcintosh, his shirt front stained with blood, his face bruised and discoloured, and the little finger of his right hand injured. When the body was turned over, the reason for the blood on his chest was apparent. A bullet had caught him in the back and taken an upward course to exit just below his left collarbone. His horse was grazing nearby, and from tracks, Kirby deduced that Mcintosh had been galloping along the trail when someone stepped out of the bush behind him and shot at him, from either a kneeling or a prone position.

Just as the constable and coroner were arranging for a wagon to take the dead man to Hazelton, a man named Gus Sampan came running up. There was, he said between excited breaths, another body on the trail about a mile and a half from Hazelton.

The second dead man was Max LeClair, also lying flat on his back. He had been killed in the same fashion as Mcintosh—hit in the back about two inches from his spine. Like Mcintosh, LeClair had been riding, and again it appeared that someone had stepped out on the trail after he passed, and then knelt and fired.

Hazelton, BC, c. 1912. BRITISH COLUMBIA ARCHIVES

To Kirby and Hicks-Beach, one thing was crystal clear: the man who did the shooting was certainly a marksman. But was it one man? How could he shoot one, then gallop to another vantage point to kill the other? Maybe there were two murderers? But then there was the coincidence of the bullet's point of impact. Rather uncanny!

In his inquiry, Kirby interviewed those who had been at the party at Two Mile. Some were evasive, some reluctant, and some had such hangovers they didn't remember a thing. Out of it all, however, came some details of the altercation between Mcintosh and Gun-an-Noot. Some were even prepared to swear they heard Gun-an-Noot threaten to kill Alec. There was also evidence that Peter Hi-ma-Dan, Gun-an-Noot's brother-in-law, had taken part in the brawl.

LeClair's death, however, was puzzling, since he hadn't been at the Two Mile shindig. A Frenchman, and a rather quiet type, he had been a seaman but settled around Hazelton and ran a pack train. Apparently he met his death while on his way to pick up some straying horses.

With these details in his notebook, Kirby visited Gun-an-Noot's cabin.

Gun-an-Noot was gone, but in the corral were four dead horses that he had apparently shot, maybe to deprive pursuers of their use. While checking the cabin, Kirby noticed that all the ammunition was gone. Gun-an-Noot's wife, Sarah, was noncommittal. Later, Kirby questioned Nah Gun, Gun-an-Noot's father, who said he didn't know a thing. Finally, late that same afternoon, Kirby got word that Peter Hi-ma-Dan had disappeared.

An inquest followed, with the jury of the opinion that the two white men were killed by Gun-an-Noot and his brother-in-law, Peter Hi-ma-Dan. Warrants were issued charging the pair with murder.

While it is a relatively simple matter to get a warrant, sometimes it is a lot more difficult to execute it. In the case of Gun-an-Noot, it was thirteen years before any policeman put a hand on him—and then he surrendered voluntarily. While this performance may seem inept on the policemen's part, their task was as difficult as chasing fish in the sea.

Gun-an-Noot, wiry and agile, was the type whose moccasined feet took him through thickets with the ease and speed of a deer and whose woodcraft was superlative. To him, the whole Omineca country from Bell-Irving River to Klua-tan-tan was an open book. It is an area as big as France, and in it he knew every river and ridge, every slough and creek, every mountain trail.

First to pursue him were Constables Jim Kirby and Maitland-Dougall. Although they followed his trail for quite a while, they finally lost it. Then they found it again, pressed on for a week, then lost it once more. All that summer of 1906, relays of police and special constables, many of them expert bushmen and trackers, scoured the country. They checked every chance clue, but never came in sight of that will-o'-the-wisp, Gun-an-Noot.

Summer merged into fall, which in turn gave way to winter. Travel now was by snowshoe and dog team, and while the latter was a little quicker than hiking on foot, somehow it didn't bring the police any nearer to the outlaws. As one police party relieved another, old sourdoughs voiced their grudging admiration for the way the fugitives were holding out, and barroom wags occasionally changed Simon's name from Gun-an-Noot to "Done-a-Scoot." Now even the police had some respect for a man who could be here, there, and everywhere, and finally nowhere at all. With this also came the realization that checking all the vague reports was a considerable drain on local police manpower.

The next spring, headquarters at Victoria finally decided that local men had better stick to their day-to-day problems while a special squad chased the outlaws. This group included Sergeant F.R. Murray, Constables Otway Wilkie and John Huggard, two guides and packers, plus two former members of the North West Mounted Police. For good measure, to these seven experienced men was added another well-known northerner, Bert Glassey.

The plan called for two parties, one to go up the Stikine and come in over the Skeena watershed, checking the Yukon Telegraph Line cabins on the way. The other party, under Wilkie, would go in from Hazelton. In fall 1907, Wilkie left Hazelton for Takla Lake, ninety-six miles (one hundred and fifty-four kilometres) away, where he established a base camp. From there he pushed to Bear Lake, reaching it on October 8. He and his party scoured part of the shoreline by raft, then went down the Bear and Sustut Rivers on an eight-day exploration and returned in a blizzard. It was a sample of the cruel conditions faced by the searchers.

January found the party up on Kitkeah Pass "nearly out of provisions, but two prospectors, Bates and Olsen, had some goat meat." They searched the Otseka and Kettle Rivers and finally returned to Bear Lake without seeing a trace of Gun-an-Noot. Some fresh blazes on trees in the Otseka country roused their interest, but when they finally found the trailblazer, he was a Fort Graham Native man.

On January 31, 1908, the frostbitten, bone-weary searchers started bucking the deep snow on the mountainous trail back to Hazelton. They struggled for ten days to cover the ninety-six miles.

The expedition could chalk up only one very slight gain. On the trail, Wilkie arrested a Native man named Skookum House Tom, alias Sam Brown, "for theft of furs and refusing to obey a summons two years ago." Just to ensure that Sam stepped right along with him, Wilkie took possession of $500 worth of furs, plus $100 in cash. There was one other interesting note in Wilkie's report. A Native man at Bear Lake told him that one of their women had found a white man's head in perfect condition, or "quite fresh," as the woman put it. The find was made near Teclapan River and remains another northern mystery.

Wilkie's report had the final suggestion that it would be better to take up the chase in summer when horses could be employed. "Either that," he said, "or give up the chase until some reliable information is received."

Though some people at the time were inclined to smirk at what they considered the ineffectual nature of Wilkie's effort, his search party had travelled over a thousand miles (sixteen hundred kilometres), mostly on foot and mostly under gruelling winter conditions. How close they were to succeeding was revealed eleven years later when Peter Hi-ma-Dan gave his version. It turned out that the Wilkie party was unwittingly pushing the fugitives pretty hard. Peter revealed that at times they faced starvation but still had to keep moving to elude the police party. Sometimes they even trained their rifles on the group, almost tempted to end the chase by wounding or killing.

After Wilkie's departure, no further organized searches were conducted for the fugitives. Season followed season, always with the stray word coming by the grapevine that Simon Gun-an-noot had been seen somewhere or another. Once there was a report that Peter Hi-ma-Dan had left him, and later still, word that Peter had drowned in rapids.

In August 1914, the outbreak of the First World War dismissed thoughts of fugitive outlaws from the public mind. Instead, young men lined up at recruiting offices, and casualty lists were of greater interest than a search for two Native men. Meantime, old-timers around Hazelton died, or left, and in the ceaseless departmental shuffling, policemen moved in and out of Hazelton. New men were replaced by still newer men, who, but for an old reward notice, had never heard of Gun-an-Noot, who was becoming a sort of legend—a far-off memory.

Now and again, around campfires or in barrooms, Robin Hood–type stories were told about him: he had slipped back to Kispiox in the dark of the moon, or had once been seen stalking the back alleys of Hazelton on some midnight visit. There was also a story that annually some Hazelton trader packed grub to a secret and distant rendezvous, then returned with Gun-an-Noot's furs. Lastly, there was the rumour that Gun-an-Noot had discovered a fabulously rich mine; the more the story was told, the richer the ore grew.

A few people accidentally met Gun-an-Noot. One was Frank Chettleburgh, who encountered Gun-an-Noot in March

1912. Chettleburgh, with his Kispiox guide, was locating some claims along the Pebble River in the Ground Hog country, one hundred and fifty miles (two hundred and forty kilometres) north of Hazelton. "I saw smoke across the valley one afternoon," he related, "so I asked my Indian who it might be."

"Just another Indian," was the somewhat evasive reply.

Chettleburgh wanted to meet the camper, but his Kispiox guide was against it. "He doesn't like white men," was all he would say.

Chettleburgh, however, headed down the trail and made the lone camper's acquaintance. "He was an Indian all right," he recalled. "Well set up, about thirty-five." He was also, despite the guide's warning, quite frank and friendly. He didn't give his name but asked who owned the cache by the river. Chettleburgh said he did. "I like one jam," said the Native man.

"Go ahead. Take what you want when you're down there," was Chettleburgh's friendly offer. A week later he found a chip of wood at the cache bearing the pencilled legend, "I take one jam."

Later, on a wet afternoon when he was making some notes, a shadow suddenly darkened Chettleburgh's tent flap. It was his chance-met Native man, bearing a hindquarter of caribou. "To pay for the jam," he said with simple dignity.

As Chettleburgh stood by his tent, watching the sturdy figure depart down the trail, his Kispiox guide remarked, "His name's Gun-an-Noot."

During the First World War, Mrs. Peter Hi-ma-Dan died at Kispiox. Before she breathed her last, however, she made a confession: she had killed Max LeClair. In her halting speech, she told how in the early hours of the morning she was on her way to Two Mile to get Peter home from the party. On the way she met LeClair.

He'd had a drink or two and put his arms around her. She pushed him away, ran to her horse, and yanked a rifle out of its scabbard. LeClair mounted and was making off when she fired to scare him. When she saw she had hit him, she started to cry. Then Gun-an-Noot, who had heard the shot, galloped up. He took her home, telling her to say nothing; he would take the blame for LeClair's death. But she must never reveal what happened on the trail that night.

"When she and Gun-an-Noot got home," she said, "Nah Gun, his father, told them that Mcintosh had also been shot and that Gun-an-Noot was sure to be blamed. He'd better go back in the mountains and stay there. It was on Nah Gun's advice," said the dying woman, "that Gun-an-Noot had taken to the hills."

The whole confession sounded unnatural. Why, if the man took off on his horse, did she have to shoot him? How could she shoot so accurately in the dark? How did Nah Gun know that Mcintosh was dead? Later, from the Native reserve, came another story. This time it was Peter Hi-ma-Dan who was drunk and shot LeClair, just as Peter's wife appeared on the scene. Thinking to protect her husband, she had taken the blame in her deathbed confession. Again there was a flaw. How could a drunk man plant a bullet in a man's back with such accuracy?

The confessions kept Gun-an-Noot's name very much alive in the Hazelton area, as did another police change that made Smithers the administrative headquarters of the district. Hazelton became a mere police post, with one man in charge. His name was Cline. Though he became Sergeant Cline to a lot of latter-day recruits in the old BC Provincial Police, and "Sperry" to his intimates, it was as "Dutch" Cline that Hazelton's pioneers knew him. His nickname originated because his bronze-tinted beard and hairy chest conjured up a likeness of a South African Dutchman.

One day in 1919, Cline was watching some of the more important records being removed to the new Smithers office. Then, with a casual sweep of his hand, Cline removed the old Gun-an-Noot reward notice that had flaunted its fly-specked challenge to every office visitor for over ten years.

Those who knew Dutch Cline were aware that he never did anything without a purpose. His reason for removing the poster was to break the intimidating spell it held over the Native people who occasionally visited the office and to start a plan he was formulating. Now that he was boss of his one-man detachment, he decided to wind up the Gun-an-Noot case.

How he was going to do it is a story that pre-dates the First World War, when he and George Beirnes were partners running the mail by dog team from Hazelton to Kitimat on the frozen Skeena. Beirnes was still around, even had a little story to impart to his former partner. He'd met Gun-an-Noot away out in the Bear country. Although at first suspicious, Gun-an-Noot thawed somewhat when Beirnes gave him word of current fur prices. It seems that rumour was right, and that Gun-an-Noot had a pal who was bringing out grub and taking away furs. But the pal was cheating him, lying about prices he was getting for fur. Gun-an-Noot felt friendly toward the white man who had wised him up, and in turn Beirnes suggested that he surrender. Gun-an-Noot looked thoughtful, then asked if it would be possible to have a lawyer.

"Sure," said Beirnes. "You tell us what day you'll come to Hazelton. We'll have a lawyer waiting to see you."

When Beirnes got back to Hazelton, he and Cline arranged for Stuart Henderson, a famous Vancouver lawyer, to act as counsel. Henderson came to Hazelton, but on the day that Gun-an-Noot was to surrender, his wife had a baby and he sent word that he had to stay with her.

Cline and Beirnes now had two problems: Henderson couldn't remain in Hazelton without arousing suspicion, and Gun-an-Noot was himself getting suspicious. Beirnes, it seems, had said something about collecting the reward and giving it to Gun-an-Noot to help defray legal costs. Gun-an-Noot was dubious about the plan. How could anyone collect a reward on him if he voluntarily gave himself up?

Simon Gun-an-Noot, centre, with lawyer Stuart Henderson, at left, and George Biernes, who suggested that the fugitive surrender.
BRITISH COLUMBIA ARCHIVES I-61617

Finally this doubt was smoothed out, and they set a new date for Gun-an-Noot to walk in. It was now Cline's turn to get the jitters. Supposing some old-timer with a long memory spotted Gun-an-Noot outside town and tried to play the hero by bringing him in at gunpoint. In this event, there could easily be another murder.

As things happened, however, Cline wasn't there for the surrender he had arranged. The day before, he was subpoenaed to give evidence in a case at Prince Rupert. As he prepared to board the train, his relief, Constable John Kelly, stepped down to the platform.

They chatted for a minute, then Cline casually

remarked, "You know, John, I wouldn't be surprised if Gun-an-Noot didn't give himself up one of these days."

Kelly, never a man for needless mirth, gave a wry smile and didn't answer. The whole thing was too ridiculous.

Next afternoon, as he stood behind the office counter making some entries in a book, a shadow-like, mocassin-clad figure suddenly stood before him. "Yes," said Kelly, looking up.

"I'm Gun-an-Noot," said the impassive stranger. "I've come to give myself up."

Before Kelly could decide whether it was a gag, Stuart Henderson and Beirnes turned up alongside the Native man.

The trial was held in Vancouver that fall. Inspector Tom Parsons of Prince George took the famous fugitive to Vancouver. When he was brought from his cell, Gun-an-Noot, blinking shyly, stuck out his wrists for handcuffs. With a smile, Parsons said, "No handcuffs."

As Stuart Henderson had anticipated, the hearing was brief. In fact, so outdated was the crime that the few people in court stole more glances at the clock than at the impassive Native man sitting in the prisoner's box. The Crown had no evidence to produce, and the verdict was not guilty. On October 8, 1918, Simon Gun-an-Noot stepped into the street, no longer a wanted man. Months later, his brother-in-law, Peter Hi-ma-Dan, took his turn in the dock. "There was not a tittle of evidence produced to connect him with either murder, and he was discharged at the preliminary hearing," Sutherland recalled.

Gun-an-Noot went back to the Skeena watershed, to the country he knew and loved. It was there he was trapping, just north of Bowser Lake, when illness overtook him in 1933. He died that October. Some of his fellow tribesmen packed his body nine miles (fourteen kilometres) to bury him beside his father on Bowser Lake. People remembered that Simon once packed his father's body forty miles (sixty-four kilometres) to do the same thing.

It was four months before Native trapper Tom Campbell brought word to the outside world that Gun-an-Noot had died. The news brought a momentary clatter to telegraph sounders from Prince Rupert to Jasper, and in every one of the lonely little cabins along the 1,500-mile-long (2,400-kilometre) Yukon Telegraph Line from Quesnel to Dawson City. Then the event was largely forgotten, except in BC's vast northwest. Even today, when old-timers meet around campfires and in living rooms in the Hazelton, Omineca, and Babine country, the legendary Gun-an-Noot lives on.

8

Phantoms of the Rangeland

THE CARIBOO REGION OF BRITISH COLUMBIA covers a sprawling plateau-like area some 200 miles (320 kilometres) long from Ashcroft in the south to Quesnel in the north, and from the silt-laden waters of the Fraser River on the west to the glacier-clad Cariboo Mountains on the east. First settled by white men during the 1860s, when the Cariboo Mountains yielded more than $100 million in gold, it evolved into ranching country with thousands of white-faced Herefords roaming its bunchgrass valleys and timbered sidehills.

But for eighteen months beginning in 1911, more than cattle were at home on the Cariboo rangeland. During this period, two killers, Native men Paul Spintlum and Moses

Paul, skillfully used the rugged gullies and tree-clad ridges to elude the men who sought to bring them to justice for the murder of three men.

The story began on a hot mid-July day in 1911 when a Cariboo freight-team driver, Louis Crosina, ran into the police office in the hamlet of Clinton and excitedly announced to Constable Jack McMillan that he had seen a dead man in Suicide Valley.

"How do you know he's dead?" asked McMillan.

"He's not only dead," said Crosina. "He's been murdered. His head's bashed in."

Promptly, McMillan rode with Crosina some four miles (six kilometres) south down the Cariboo Wagon Road to the valley, appropriately named since it had been the scene of three suicides. Here he found the remains of a teamster called William Whyte. Just as Crosina had said, it looked like murder. Nearby was a bloodstained rock that matched the injuries at the back of Whyte's skull.

The body lay partly concealed by a log some distance from the road and could only have been seen by someone riding on a wagon. From its condition, McMillan estimated the corpse had been lying there about three days. After searching for further clues, he arranged for the removal of the body to Clinton.

In the course of subsequent inquiries, McMillan learned from the Clinton postmaster that Whyte had been driving a team for Billy Parker at Big Lake. When he was laid off, he had been waiting in Clinton for his wages, which were due to arrive by the first stagecoach. "His letter didn't come," said the postmaster, "and he seemed pretty disappointed."

McMillan learned more by chance from Chew Wye, a Chinese wood chopper who lived in a cabin near Four Mile Lake. A week before, Chew told McMillan, Whyte had stopped in for a moment. He was a little drunk, and had a bottle of whisky in his pocket. As he was leaving, a Native man on horseback appeared from a nearby bush. Whyte gave him a drink, then climbed up behind him, and the pair rode off.

"Did you know the Indian?" asked McMillan.

"Sure," said Chew. "It was Moses Paul."

McMillan knew Paul, a rangy twenty-five-year-old who had never been in trouble with the law. In fact, he had taught McMillan's young daughter, Sadie, how to ride. McMillan was reluctant to accept the possibility that Paul had anything to do with Whyte's death. Nevertheless, he paid Moses Paul a visit and was surprised to find him singularly reticent. He merely stated that after a couple of drinks, he and Whyte had parted a few miles from Chew's cabin. However, while searching Paul's cabin, McMillan found a watch in the loft.

The discovery of the watch convinced McMillan that Moses Paul might have been involved in Whyte's murder. He took Paul to Clinton's jail—a building that had seen little use since the last murder had been committed twenty years before—and continued his investigations.

Constable McMillan became convinced that Moses Paul (above) was involved in the murder of William Whyte. BRITISH COLUMBIA ARCHIVES C-05792

A few days later, while McMillan was getting in some hay, Paul escaped.

McMillan soon learned that Paul Spintlum, a friend of Moses Paul, had recently purchased a stock of groceries and rifle ammunition at Bob Fraser's store. Could he be the one who had helped Moses Paul escape? If so, McMillan now had two men to chase, both Chilcotin Native men who knew the country like a book, were adept at covering their tracks, and were probably able to get help from friends and relatives. Furthermore, he strongly suspected that Moses Paul had murdered William Whyte, since the watch he found in Paul's loft had been identified as belonging to the dead teamster.

A few weeks later, McMillan's suspicions were confirmed when Ah Joe, a friend of woodcutter Chew Wye, called at Chew's cabin. There was no sign of life, no wisp of smoke from the tin smokestack. Pushing open the door, Ah Joe was shocked to see his friend lying on the floor, his head covered in blood. A bloodstained axe lay beside him.

Ah Joe trotted the four miles into Clinton to tell his incoherent story to Constable McMillan. Surveying the cabin shortly afterward, McMillan felt sure the killer was someone known to Chew Wye, in order to be able to hit him from behind with his own axe. Outside, McMillan found the tracks of two men who had stood on a small knoll overlooking the cabin, probably waiting for Chew Wye's return. They had to be Paul and Spintlum—one of them getting rid of the witness to Paul's association with the murdered Whyte.

McMillan wired details to Chief Constable Joe Burr some twenty miles (thirty-two kilometres) away at Ashcroft. Burr arrived on the next stagecoach with three constables. After the inquest, which reached the verdict of "murdered by person or persons unknown," the search for the fugitives continued.

Like will-o'-the-wisps, they were reported here, then there, then somewhere else, only to vanish before the police arrived. After weeks of relentless searching, the police realized that their biggest handicap was the aid given to the two fugitives by fellow tribesmen. They were being supplied not with food, shelter, and fresh horses, but also with information about the movements of their pursuers.

The best chance for the police was to keep the pair on the run and hope for a lucky break. But months passed with no sign of the men. McMillan had now been superseded by Constable Lee, who, after a few months, resigned from the force. His place was taken by a young Scot, Constable Alec Kindness. When the spring assizes opened in Clinton on May 3, 1912, nearly a year had passed since Whyte's murder. The police had not even seen the wanted pair, let alone arrested them.

The assizes were always an event of great interest in small communities. Clinton was no different, and that morning, as a group of townsmen smoked and gossiped outside the courthouse, their attention was suddenly drawn to a lone horseman galloping into town. His arrival signalled the break the police had been waiting for.

The rider was Charlie Truran, a homesteader employed at nearby Pollard's Ranch who that morning had been searching for a couple of strayed horses. After crossing Mile 51 Creek, he had spotted a pair of horses downstream under some trees. As he rode up close, two men leaped from the underbrush, each grabbing a rifle.

It was then, Truran said, that he realized he was looking at Paul and Spintlum. The fugitives eyed him stonily, and Truran pretended not to recognize them.

"I lost a couple of horses. You fellows seen them?"

Truran's question was met with stolid indifference.

"If you see them," he said, "let me know and I'll give you $10." It was a handsome offer, since the going rate for returning a strayed horse was $2.50.

"Okay," said one of the outlaws with a smirk. "If we find them, we'll let you know."

Truran turned his horse and, not without a sense of fear, slowly walked away. Once out of sight, he applied his spurs and galloped into Clinton.

On hearing the story, Constable Kindness at once formed a posse consisting of Jimmy Boyd and Bill Ritchie of Clinton, Constable Forest Loring, an assize witness from Ashcroft, and George Carson of Pavilion. Armed with Winchesters, they galloped to Pollard's Ranch, where Charlie Pollard joined them. At this point, Truran's enthusiasm for the chase waned, and his place was taken by Johnny, the rancher's son.

When the riders reached the trees where Truran had met the outlaws, a quick look around showed the direction in which they had gone. Pressing on at full gallop, the posse soon overtook a pack horse, its lead rope dragging.

"Come on, boys, we're crowding 'em," yelled Boyd. "They've had to drop that horse."

Then, leaning over to Kindness, he suggested the

constable drop to the rear. "I know these fellows," he said. "They won't hurt me, but you're a policeman. They'll shoot you sure as hell."

Kindness grinned acknowledgment but retained his lead position. The consequence would be tragic.

Almost before the horsemen knew it, they rounded a bend in the trail and came to a hoof-stamping halt in front of some trees felled by the wind. A rifle cracked from behind the fallen timber. Kindness slumped forward in his saddle, then slid to the ground, dead.

Two more shots rang out as the posse milled around in confusion. Loring felt a hammer blow to his wrist as a bullet broke it. Boyd dismounted and pumped shot after shot at the outlaw's hideout. Loring, clasping his wrist, moved out of range, while Ritchie risked the fusillade to pull Kindness's body to shelter.

Ritchie said later that when he realized Kindness was dead, he looked up in time to see Boyd, who had run out of ammunition, bravely charging toward the outlaws. He was ready to use his gun as a club. Fortunately, the fugitives had vanished.

With the murder of Constable Kindness, the police realized they were dealing with cold-blooded killers. The head of the BC Provincial Police force, Superintendent Colin S. Campbell, arrived at Clinton and immediately wired to Kamloops for Chief Constable W.L. Fernie to join him. Fernie brought with him Alphonse Ignace, a Shuswap Native man known for his tracking ability, and six helpers. Fernie was to state later, "For skill in tracking, I'd place those Shuswaps with the world's best."

About three weeks after the death of Kindness, Al Neas, a rancher at Big Bar Creek northwest of Clinton, rode over to fellow rancher Bill Janes at Desolation Ranch to get a horse. Although they were only eighteen miles (twenty-nine kilometres) from Clinton, neither had heard about the policeman's murder. Neas stayed overnight with his friend, and in the morning went out to the barn to find that his saddle was missing. He asked if Janes had moved it.

"Never touched it," was his friend's response.

The pair returned to the barn to have another look. The saddle peg was near an open window, and as they speculated where the saddle might have gone, they heard a movement in the yard. It was Fernie and his trackers.

It was then the pair heard the story of the Clinton killing and how Fernie and his men had trailed the fugitives for twenty-one days. One of the outlaws, they reported, was mounted, the other on foot. Sometimes one ran beside the horse, occasionally both were mounted. As the tracks led to the barn, it was obvious they had taken the saddle.

From Desolation Ranch, the tracks led into the turfy Big Bar Lake country. From there the trail turned north, then west, and alternated across high ridges so that the fugitives could scan the back country with field glasses stolen from another rancher. It led into the Rafael Lake country, then back to Big Bar, and later, from a ridge, down toward the Fraser River and the Canoe Creek Indian Reserve. At the reserve, Fernie's questions brought evasive answers or obstinate silence.

The trail now led into boulder-strewn country. Here, on one occasion, Fernie began to doubt the reliability of his Native helpers. Even though Alphonse was uncannily clever in reading trail signs, Fernie finally suggested that he may have lost the trail. Alphonse gave a fleeting smile and cantered down a dry creek bed into a patch of cottonwoods. He pointed to hoof marks, then, scanning the shoulder-high willows nearby, singled out a leaf for Fernie's inspection. One leaf. But it bore a faint black smudge from being rubbed by a fire-blackened cooking pot slung on a saddle.

The next day, the trackers came so suddenly on the outlaws' camp that their fire was still burning briskly. That Paul and Spintlum had fled in great haste was proven by the flour, rice, and sugar they left behind. Fernie and his men spurred after them, but were soon baffled by a confusion of horse tracks on the trail.

"They herd wild horses ahead of them to cover tracks. Old Indian trick," explained the sagacious Alphonse. It took the best part of a day to pick up the trail, and then it led toward the Bonaparte River.

Near Fish Lake, a hundred miles (one hundred and sixty kilometres) south of Canoe Creek Reserve, the pursuers discovered that they were not far behind their quarry. They found an abandoned horse that had been stolen, then learned of another one stolen to replace it. Fernie estimated that he was only some fourteen hours behind the pair, but he was worried. If the outlaws reached the vast, mountainous Clearwater country to the northeast, the chase could go on for years.

As weeks passed, the fugitives were reported in Empire Valley, then at Big Fish Lake, where Fernie thought he saw a movement on an island in the lake. There was a little scow-type boat nearby, so he and Alphonse paddled over to the island. There had been movement, true enough, but it was caused by the island's only inhabitant—a buck deer.

Toward the end of summer came a report that the outlaws had been seen at Porcupine Creek above Kelly Lake in the southern Cariboo. A Native tracker, Cultus Jack, trailed them to Jimmy Wood's place, then lost the trail high up on a stony ridge. They'd been there, all right, but had vanished like smoke.

A week later, Bill Pearson of the Kelly Lake Ranch reported seeing two saddled horses standing near the lake and figured the wanted men had jumped into the bush to escape notice. Old Strawnick, Moses Paul's mother, was friendly with the Pearsons and pleaded with Mrs. Pearson not to let her son join the chase.

"He be killed for sure," she warned, adding that on the day Paul broke jail, she had put a curse on the police.

Curse or no curse, the chase went on until it became clear that the outlaws had either crossed the Fraser and gone into the Camelsfoot Range, or crossed Kelly Lake into the Hat Creek country. Two constables searched without results, but they did learn that the Nicola Natives would have nothing to do with the killers. This rejection might mean that the outlaws had been forced into the hills near Hat Creek.

By now it was fall, and snow would soon shroud the Cariboo. The police decided on a fresh approach. They had scoured thousands of square miles of undulating rangeland, crossed scores of creeks, and spent months on the trail. While they had come tantalizingly close to the murderers, they had yet to see either one, although the incredible skill shown by the Native trackers in following the circuitous, indistinct trail became a legend in the cattle country.

On November 15, Chief Constable Burr spoke with several Native chiefs, pointing out that support of law and order was both white people's and Native people's business. If they wanted future support from the law, then their people would have to stop assisting those who had so callously murdered three men. The chiefs seemed to see the wisdom in this statement and asked for a month in which to talk it over with their people.

Word soon drifted into Clinton that a lot of parleying was going on among the Native people. The talks appeared to be bringing a favourable result, for indications were that the outlaws were going to be handed over.

On December 15, 1912, Burr got in touch with Thomas Cummiski, then superintendent of Indian agencies for British Columbia. He asked to hold a meeting with the chiefs and get their collective answer, pointing out that a month had gone by and it was time for action. He also suggested that if

Chief Constable J.W. Burr asked
for the co-operation of the Native
chiefs in handing over the outlaws.
BRITISH COLUMBIA ARCHIVES F-07350

the chiefs did not co-operate, they should be deposed and
new ones appointed.

Cummiski agreed and subsequently reported that he
had arranged a meeting near Ashcroft, where the outlaws
would be handed over. But there were conditions. The
killers were not to be handcuffed. They were to be provided
with legal counsel. In addition, medals were to be presented
to the chiefs who had engineered the surrender as an
indication of their support for law and order.

In the late afternoon of December 30, Superintendent Cummiski, accompanied by six selected chiefs, went to the Bonaparte Reserve near Ashcroft. With no police present and with little ceremony, Paul and Spintlum were handed over to Cummiski. The eighteen-month rangeland pursuit had ended without further loss of life.

There was a standing reward of $3,000 for the capture of the murderers, and the BC government thought it was a good idea to split the money among the chiefs. They refused. "There's blood on it," was their opinion.

In accordance with the agreement, the government had six impressive medals made, each inscribed with a chief's name and brief details of how he had earned it. When presentation day came, however, the chiefs refused them. The medals, still brightly new, are today in the Provincial Archives in Victoria.

The prisoners were escorted to the Kamloops jail, both showing obvious signs of the hardships they had undergone. After two trials—one at Vernon, the other at New Westminster—Moses Paul was found guilty of murder, and Spintlum adjudged an accessory after the fact. Paul was hanged at the Kamloops jail on December 12, 1913, while Spintlum, suffering from tuberculosis, died soon after starting a life sentence. Thus closed the saga of the longest manhunt in the history of the Cariboo. It was a hunt that justified Constable Fernie's faith in his Native trackers—the men he placed "with the world's best."

Selected Bibliography

Books

Baillie-Grohman, W.A. *Fifteen Years' Sport and Life in the Hunting Grounds of Western America and British Columbia*. London: Horace Cox, 1900.

Birney, Hoffman. *Vigilantes*. New York: Grosset & Dunlap, 1929.

Clark, Cecil. *B.C. Provincial Police Stories*. Surrey, BC: Heritage House, 1999.

Cornwallis, Kinahan. *The New El Dorado; or, British Columbia*. London: Thomas Cautley Newby, 1858.

Drumheller, D.M. *"Uncle Dan" Drumheller Tells Thrills of Western Trails in 1854*. Spokane, WA: Inland-Association Printing Co., 1925.

Grant, George M., Rev. *Ocean to Ocean: Sandford Fleming's Expedition Through Canada in 1872*. Toronto, London: James Campbell & Son, 1873.

Langford, Nathanial Pitt. *Vigilante Days and Ways: The Pioneers of the Rockies*. Boston: J.G. Cupples Co., 1890.

Walkem, W.W. *Stories of Early British Columbia*. Vancouver: *News-Advertiser*, 1914.

Williams, David R. *The Man For a New Country: Sir Matthew Baillie Begbie*. Sidney, BC: Gray's Publishing, 1977.

Newspapers
The British Columbian
Jefferson City Inquirer
Mainland Guardian (New Westminster)
The Prospector (Fort Steele)
The Times (London)
The Toronto Mail
Victoria Colonist
Victoria Daily Times

List of Authors

Index

Index